# HIGHER EDUCATION
## and the
# FEDERAL
# GOVERNMENT

# HIGHER EDUCATION
## AND THE FEDERAL GOVERNMENT

### Programs and Problems

PAPERS PRESENTED AT THE
FORTY-FIFTH ANNUAL MEETING
CHICAGO · OCTOBER 3–5, 1962

*Edited by* CHARLES G. DOBBINS

AMERICAN COUNCIL ON EDUCATION
*Washington, D.C.*

# FOREWORD

THE EXPANDING RELATIONSHIPS BETWEEN HIGHER EDUCATION AND THE Federal Government deserve and are receiving wide attention among both educators and public officials. With financial problems of the institutions requiring added support from all sources, including the Federal Government, and with new demands being made on colleges and universities for services in the national interest, these relationships are certain to grow in number and complexity.

Federal officials have shown a concern with these common problems quite commensurate with that of leaders in education. The American Council on Education recognizes, however, that even with the best of spirit and intent in Government and education, meeting grounds must be provided for presentation of issues, for projection of goals, and for agreement on approaches to problems. The Council accepts responsibility for a major role in providing such meeting places. The staff endeavors to maintain regular liaison with Congress and the relevant Federal executive agencies. The Council arranges meetings for specific purposes between representatives of higher education and the Federal Government. Concentration of the 1962 Annual Meeting of the Council on "Higher Education and the Federal Government: Programs and Problems," with important participation by Government spokesmen, was in recognition of a mutuality of interest.

In this volume, which presents the major addresses from the 1962 meeting, it will be noted that educators acknowledged the need for better awareness, articulation, and organization in the colleges and universities, and that Federal officials stressed the responsibility of Government and the public for financial support and better understanding of the fundamental role of the institutions. We believe that the candor and objectivity of these utterances serve the nation well.

LOGAN WILSON, *President*
*American Council on Education*

# INTRODUCTION

SERIOUS PROBLEMS UNDOUBTEDLY EXIST IN THE RELATIONS OF HIGHER education with the Federal Government, but they are the product of substantial common concerns, and can be solved. This conclusion seems to emerge from the papers in this volume presented by educators and public officials at the 1962 Annual Meeting of the American Council on Education.

There were other notes of encouragement in the sessions, too. One was the evident agreement, up to the highest level of Government, that the welfare of colleges and universities is essential to the nation's welfare and, therefore, that adequate support for higher education is one of the nation's responsibilities. When President John F. Kennedy extended greetings to members of the American Council on October 4, he said:

> The national interest and the welfare of higher education are closely intertwined. The nation turns to your institutions for the education of highly trained technicians and professional manpower, for fresh discovery through research, and for advice on the conduct of public affairs. Our free society depends on the diversified study and rigorous inquiry that strong colleges and universities provide. . . . This administration will continue to support your vigorous efforts to secure the resources critically needed to provide the quality and quantity of educational opportunity demanded by both America's heavy responsibilities and its ideals of intellectual excellence.

Another encouragement was the assurance, presented at several points, that with consultation, careful planning, and adequate safeguards, major Federal programs of assistance to higher education can be highly successful. Examples were cited at one of the general sessions when, as presiding officer, Dr. Theodore A. Distler, executive director of the Association of American Colleges, honored two men at the speaker's table in the following words:

*To Mr. Sidney H. Woolner, Commissioner, Community Facilities Administration, Housing and Home Finance Agency:*

> Whenever college and university people think of successful partnership between higher education and the Federal Government, they cannot possibly omit the College Housing Loan Program . . .

Nearly everybody is familiar with the remarkable history of this partnership enterprise of Government and higher education extending over 12 years, under the administration of three Presidents. It was recently reported that 70 percent, or 953 out of the 1,366 eligible colleges and universities, have applied for loans. More than $2 billion has been approved for these loans. In fact, one out of every three students in a college dormitory this fall lives in a building financed by the College Housing Program. We are proud, of course, that the record shows no college has ever defaulted!

A successful program like this does not just happen. It is the result of good planning, good administration, and good faith. We thank you, Mr. Woolner, and through you we thank our Federal Government for this wise, timely, capably directed program of assistance to higher education.

*To Dr. Alan T. Waterman, Director, National Science Foundation:*

Your distinguished career as a professor at Yale and as chief scientist of the Office of Naval Research was a worthy prelude to your service as the first director of the National Science Foundation. In that capacity you have guided the development of a prime organ of our national purpose over a period in which its growth has been reflected by the expansion of its budget from $3½ million to $300 million.

Your administration of the Foundation has been consistently inspired by a clear vision of our national need both for scientific progress and for public understanding of its role. You have campaigned vigorously and courageously for improvement of basic research and graduate education in the sciences. Your unyielding demand for excellence has uplifted the aspirations and achievements of American scientists. You have constantly reminded our people of the social value of scientific endeavor, of the men and women who engage in it and of the institutions in which it is carried on.

And, with all this, you have never been unmindful of the national interest in the healthy growth of other disciplines and the maintenance of a proper balance between science and the humanities. All in all, your work for scientific development has contributed significantly to the strengthening of our institutions of higher education and through them to our national well-being.

The Council, through its Commission on Federal Relations, is working for the spirit of mutual concern and helpfulness in the area of Government and higher education which was cited by Dr. Distler. We are grateful for the contribution which the papers in this volume make to an extension of this spirit and to the solution of some of our problems.

CHARLES G. DOBBINS, *Director,*
*Commission on Federal Relations*

# TABLE OF CONTENTS

# A TIME FOR ASSESSMENT

*Herbert E. Longenecker*

PRESIDENT, TULANE UNIVERSITY

D URING THIS YEAR WE HAVE JOINED IN THE NATION'S SALUTE TO ITS land-grant institutions of higher education and with them have celebrated the centennial of the first Morrill Act. The exercise has served as a reminder that the Federal Government has long had an involvement in the affairs of higher education. In fact, it dates back to the earliest days of the newly organized government in the late 1700's. But it has also, and perhaps more importantly, served to underscore the changed situation of the present-day involvement of the Federal Government with nearly all institutions of higher education.

## The Nature of Federal Involvement in Higher Education

The traditionally close ties of the land-grant colleges with the Federal Government have been maintained and strengthened through annual subsidies for general support and through programs for agricultural research and extension. But these institutions have experienced, along with the non-land-grant institutions an even greater and far more extensive participation in Federal relationships than those provided for in the first and second Morrill Acts or in Public Law 658 of July 1960, which authorized substantial increases in land-grant college subsidies. For the non-land-grant institutions—both public and private, large and small, church-related and completely independent— involvement in relationships with the Federal Government has emerged as a completely new dimension in education within the past two decades. During earlier periods of national crisis, spasmodic relationships were encountered as, for example, in the training of additional military officers in World War I and in the public works and personal economic assistance programs of the 1930's.

For the totality of higher education, it is difficult to state with accuracy the full extent of the present involvement. In fiscal terms, Government-sponsored research in colleges and universities exceeds one billion dollars per year and the total Federal Government expenditures for all programs carried on in these institutions approximate twice that amount.

Governmental research expenditures involve directly only a small proportion of the colleges and universities of the nation and about half of these expenditures are for major contract research centers. But all institutions are affected by the expanded rate of acquisition of new knowledge and by the number and kinds of persons prepared for teaching careers in the expanded research settings. Other governmental programs broaden the base of involved institutions substantially through the provision of student fellowships and loans, grants to support improvement of specific teaching programs, construction loans for housing and related facilities, matching grants for health research or science research facilities, ROTC, and many other programs. Of the two thousand institutions of higher education in the country, fewer than four hundred have no direct participation in Federal programs. They are primarily theological schools, proprietary schools, small undergraduate or junior colleges.

On the Government side, the involvement with institutions of higher education extends far beyond the one Federal agency which has education as a primary mission. More than a dozen major agencies have operating programs that fall into dozens of categories too numerous to detail here.

In the discussions generated by the American Assembly on "The Federal Government and Higher Education," it was evident to many participants that there were widespread misunderstandings that reflected inadequate knowledge of the present state of affairs. More than a few participants were disposed at the outset to the position that the Federal Government should have no role in higher education. They soon realized, however, the inadequacies of their position as they confronted the reality of the existing relationships, the importance of them, and the extent and directions of their growth.

Substantial misunderstanding is created by those who blanket the total interrelationship as aid to education. Such oversimplification fails to take account of the varied and evolving purposes, programs, and procedures of both the governmental agencies and the institutions of higher education. Federal programs have characteristically been quite specific. No agency of Government has been directed by congressional mandate to provide general support of education. It is within the framework of the agency's assigned mission that the institution's services have been provided for by contract or grant.

Only a few Federal programs to date have involved a wide participation by the colleges and universities. Concentration of attention on competence in scientific research at the graduate and advanced levels in selected fields has limited the number of institutions. Likewise within strongly participating institutions, Federal funds are largely concentrated in the natural sciences, engineering, and medicine.

## Institutional Outlays in Federally Sponsored Programs

For the participating institutions, the record is abundantly clear that federally sponsored programs require considerable outlays of space, facilities, funds, and constructive energy by the institution itself. Indeed, it is in many instances quite appropriate to ask which party is providing the assistance in greater measure. Not infrequently the actual dollars transferred by the Federal agency must be matched to some extent by the receiving institution. But beyond such specific requirements are the often uncounted costs represented by the institution's continuing commitment for support of research and graduate education.

For those institutions vitally affected by arbitrary restrictions of indirect cost reimbursements, there is some satisfaction in the congressional action that resulted during the past session in a modest increase in the reimbursement rate. But the very debates leading to the increase produced a welter of statements indicative of the urgent need to improve understanding of the nature of the relationships between the Federal Government and higher education.

Mixed viewpoints on the matter of cost-sharing deserve the keen attention of all institutions, including the many not now engaged in Federal programs around which the present issues are centered. Patterns and attitudes set in the present areas of engagement are easily transferred to the other areas, as again demonstrated in the past congressional session in the case of the academic facilities bill.

A recent announcement from the Department of Health, Education, and Welfare states the case directly. A new Cooperative Research and Demonstration Grant Program of the Social Security Administration[1] is intended to provide grants to support "a broad range of research of significance to social security programs and social welfare." Public agencies or nonprofit organizations are declared eligible to apply on a basis that specifically prescribes cost-sharing. The announcement of the program states: "The amount to be supplied by an applicant (institution) is not specified in the authorizing legislation. To assure that a maximum number of projects are supported by available Federal funds it is expected that each applicant (agency or institution) will finance as large a part of the project cost as possible."

In sharp contrast with this concept are some of the programs of agencies such as the National Science Foundation, the National Institutes of Health, and the Office of Education that seek to provide broad assistance to the institution within the specifically applicable fields of interest and authorizations of these agencies.

## *Policies and Programs To Strengthen Higher Education*

Clearly, policies and programs must be developed that strengthen rather than weaken the conditions of higher educational institutions. Faced with increasing responsibilities for service in the national interest, we can ill afford the luxury of a complacent attitude toward a relationship that has grown enormously in a few short years and presents prospects for further substantial enlargement. In the constantly changing balance of relationships, it is not surprising that strains have developed. Indeed, the remarkable fact is that despite the problems created by the relationship, so much of enduring value has resulted as to make it a foregone conclusion that the relationship will grow.

[1] "Social Security Cooperative Research and Demonstration Grant Program," Announcement of the Research Grants Branch, Division of Program Research, Social Security Administration, U.S. Department of Health, Education, and Welfare, August 1962.

Given these circumstances, there is a growing need for each institution to assess fully the extent and impact of the relationship upon the institution itself. A few institutions have attempted internal study on their own initiative as a part of the cooperative studies encouraged by the Carnegie Foundation for the Advancement of Teaching. Reports at this meeting will provide specific examples of individual institutional assessment. Likewise, a series of books and reports recently published, or about to appear, provide an improved basis for understanding. But excellent and helpful as these studies and reports are, they represent only a beginning toward the desired assessment of the impact of Federal Government programs in higher educational institutions.

Fortunately, a growing number of officials in Government are prepared to direct their energies toward a resolution of relationships that will give greater assurance to the whole enterprise of higher education. They are well aware of the uneven, often uncoordinated, pattern of Federal agency involvement with the colleges and universities and of the extensive influences of their programs on the objectives and operations of the institutions. And they are prepared for continuing review of their own policies and procedures.

It is evident, however, that each agency formulates its own policies and procedures and establishes its own relationship with institutions of higher education. In the one instance of an attempt to introduce a single guiding policy, namely, in respect to reimbursement for indirect costs of sponsored research under the provisions of the revised Circular A-21, there continue to be frustrations as noted above. For a maximum achievement from the pluralistic interrelationships now existing, greater effort toward policy and program coordination within the Government itself is essential.

As the institutions of higher education seek to resolve their individual and collective problems involved by interactions with the Federal Government, it seems timely to consider the means available to them for expression of their views. On what issues, for example, is it appropriate for individual institutions or specialized associations representing particular disciplines in professions to represent higher education? Can any one organization provide a means of coordination of higher education's pluralistic approaches to Government? For the American Council on Education, it is of the utmost importance to consider how its broadly representative organization can improve its procedures for appropriate representation of the needs of higher educational institutions and of the viewpoints of its members on specific points at issue.

As we seek in this meeting to consider the broad implications of the Federal Government's growing involvement in the affairs of higher education, we are mindful of the rapidly changing scene in which we work. We are mindful also of the urgent necessity for action that will lead to a more meaningful relationship between higher education and the Federal Government. Perhaps overriding all else in our thoughts is the question posed with increasing urgency: By what means other than those available within the Federal Government can our obligation for the immediate future be met?

The prospect of doubled enrollments within a decade requires immediate and sizable plant capacity and the recruitment and training of college teachers on a progressively larger scale. To operate the expanded facilities and services will require funds vastly beyond income from present sources, and the gap is not likely to be bridged by increased donations and tuitions, however essential they are. And means must be found not only for these additions but also for long overdue improvements in the level of current operational payments for faculty salaries, library and departmental expenses, building maintenance, and student services.

When, more than a year ago, agreement was reached among the institutions of higher education that the urgency of the situation made Federal action of some sort desirable, the decision was made to join in support of a program for funds for plant expansion in preference to operating budgets. A persuasive case was made for a program of loans and grants available at their option to all accredited institutions.

As you know, the proposed legislation has met a discouraging response after an ambitious start in the second session of the Eighty-seventh Congress. Was this because too large an appropriation was asked? (Many of us felt the proposals were too modest in relation to proven need.) Was it because the student financial aid question was intermingled with the facilities bill? Was it because we sought to provide opportunity for all qualified institutions to participate? What will it take to accomplish a realization that Congress' failure to act will simply confront us with that much larger a storehouse of accumulated needs and frustrations for all concerned, as we are forced to temporize another year?

Can we, at this point, restate our needs for prompt Federal action to resolve the issues that have blocked a constructive program for higher education? And can this be done with understanding that positive action for our physical needs will not solve our fiscal and personnel problems but rather will serve only to encourage our continuing efforts to close the widening gap in operational expenses by other means?

Surely, any inability to marshal our resources at this stage can only result in a continuance of legislation in bits and pieces instead of providing the basis for strengthening all segments of higher education. The discussions in this meeting can point the directions of desired action. And action is imperative at this point if we are to keep open the doors of opportunity for the nation's youth and meet fully the expectations placed on us.

# EDUCATIONAL VALUES
# AND NATIONAL PURPOSES

### Harlan Cleveland
ASSISTANT SECRETARY OF STATE
FOR INTERNATIONAL ORGANIZATION AFFAIRS

W HEN PRESIDENT EISENHOWER ASKED A DISTINGUISHED GROUP OF CITI-
zens to form a Commission on National Goals two years ago, the
result was instructive if not surprising. After one hundred papers were
prepared and several meetings held, what did the Commission come
up with?

The Declaration of Independence!

When they came right down to it, they held these truths to be self-
evident: that all men are created equal, that they are endowed by their
Creator with certain unalienable Rights, that among these are Life,
Liberty and the pursuit of Happiness; that to secure these rights, Governments are instituted among Men, deriving their just powers from
the consent of the governed.

Is this a "national purpose"? Certainly the ideas in that remarkable
document were such successful revolutionary doctrine that they are
now quite respectable, if not universally respected. But they are general ideas; they are not an action program. They add up to a vision:
almost too bright in the middle to be seen, much too fuzzy around the
edges to be defined.

Thus is our national purpose the jagged parts of ideas, the mysteri-
ous feelings of how men should arrange matters between men and the
state, of what life should be like, and could be like in the United States
with God's help and a great deal of hard work—the quantum of God's
help depending, of course, on the amount of hard work.

We did not think too much at first about exporting these ideas about
rights and consent and government. We were busy with manifest
destiny, the expansion of our territory from sea to shining sea, and

later a few islands beyond. Those who felt that territorial destiny should be as universal as the ideas in the Declaration were so exceptional they are now regarded as curiosities and relegated to the footnotes of history books—which are sometimes the most readable parts of them.

There was, for example, a Congressman Davis of Mississippi, who thought that ". . . We may expand so as to include the whole world. Mexico, Central America, South America, Cuba, the West India Islands, and even England and France [we] might annex without inconvenience or prejudice, allowing them with their local legislatures to regulate their local affairs in their own way. And this, Sir, is the mission of this Republic and its ultimate destiny."

And there was a toast allegedly given in Paris during the Civil War, which probably stands as the ultimate in American ambitions: "I give you the United States—bounded on the north by the Aurora Borealis, on the south by the procession of the equinoxes, on the east by primeval chaos and on the west by the Day of Judgment."

Most Americans were prepared to settle for something short of the equinoxes, and sooner than the Day of Judgment. If Americans were ambitious to sell Jefferson's ideas to "all men," as the Declaration said it, it was after all an abstract ambition. Mostly we wanted to be left alone. On the rattlesnake flag, the motto was in English: "Don't Tread on Me." On the pine-tree flag for the upper-class intelligentsia, the same thought appeared in Latin: "Noli me tangere." The Monroe Doctrine said the same thing, but it said it for the whole Western Hemisphere and it said so in language that all Europe—including the czar —could understand. There were a few little adventures with Big Sticks, but mostly we stayed home, in thought and deed.

## American Attitudes toward International Affairs

Then came the first threatening brush with internationalism, the war to end wars. We fought to make the world safe for the Fourteen Points, we debated the League of Nations, and we decided it was all too complicated. We were back then to the normalcy of neutrality, the disengagement from other people's troubles—we would pack ours up in the old kit bag and smile, smile, smile.

Suddenly disengagement as a national purpose—if you can call it a purpose—vanished, replaced by the brilliantly reciprocal concept of a loan for a lease, a string of bases for a fleet of destroyers. A day of infamy and four years of unconditional commitment, and we finally became, at least in name, a nation of internationalists.

The center of gravity in American politics shifted abruptly, surprisingly. Some of the same people who had tried to keep America out of two wars now could hardly wait to put the whole world together in the right way. They had no patience with the moderate majority which had never really thought we could be completely isolated and now could not bring itself to think that we could be completely involved. Curiously, the newest converts to internationalism were the most extreme and the least tolerant. In the search for the simple answer, their recommended policies came in cycles, first up and then down. First, "We must go to the Yalu" and beyond; then, "We must get out of Korea" because we are tired of it all. First, "We must have a showdown" with Communist China; then, "We must disengage" from these pushmipullyu crises in Southeast Asia.

The cyclical character of this thinking resulted, of course, from the fruitless search for the simple answer, the effort to formulate neat two-sided alternatives.

This up-down, black-and-white view of American foreign policy was often associated with a pathological fear of the Communists—not of what they actually were doing but of what they had said they would do. As the easy idealism of the late 1940's eroded over the years, it was replaced by the equally easy defeatism of the late fifties. The Communists must be doing wonderfully well, some people kept saying. Their victory is inevitable. Khrushchev, said a national magazine last year, has the world by the tail on a downhill pull.

I like to think that we have made a good deal of progress in the past year or so in shaking off what, for awhile, looked dangerously like a national mood of despair. We seem to be hearing rather less these days about the steady advance of communism and the steady retreat of the West. The demonstration that forty-five nations can become independent—it will be forty-six next Tuesday—without any of them choosing the Communists as leaders or Marxism as a way of government, has begun to sink in. Some of the popular interpreters of the Kremlin's designs are blinking away the hypnosis induced by the prophecies of these Communist prophets they want us all to read.

In short, I think there is evidence that the apocalyptic vision of triumphant, aggressive communism on the march around the world— that left-wing doctrine paradoxically so attractive to the radical right— is being dissipated by the stubborn independence of most of mankind. More and more of the world's little people are insisting, more and more loudly, on their unalienable rights. The British Foreign Secretary, Lord Home, said it well in his U.N. speech the other day: "If imperialism is being thrown out of the window on the wind of change, so is Karl Marx—and good riddance too. It is time we got rid of these obsolete reactionary doctrines of the Nineteenth Century."

## Frustrations in International Affairs

But avoiding defeatism is only half the problem. The other half is to avoid falling into the trap of acute frustration. Let us shoot down the doctrine of the downhill pull but, at the same time, let us remember we will not have the world by the tail, either. The sources of frustration will remain with us—no longer a fear of losing the cold war, but of not being able to "win" it quickly and decisively. The sources of frustration will remain so long as we are deeply enmeshed in every one of the dozens of pesky problems which make the world dangerous and uncomfortable and demanding of our time and attention and resources.

What is the trouble here, anyway? What are the roots of our present frustrations?

Some of them are as old as our history, or at least the history we are sometimes taught. The American story is a success story. Perhaps we have come as a people to believe that it is natural and right that things in this world should go as we would like them to go. Back in the early days we knew where we were going: We were going West with a whoop and a holler, and if we found primeval chaos there, we were going to fix that too.

With this practical kind of optimism built deep into our culture, we are naturally having a little trouble getting used to the fact that there isn't an American solution to every problem, even though there is an American involvement in almost every problem. The frustrating effect of this long memory is compounded by the frustrating effect of a shorter memory, hardly more than a dozen years old. We are still, I think, suffering from the illusions produced by the turn of history that made the United States the pre-eminent global power at the end of World War II.

Among the major powers, only the United States and Canada came out of the war physically undamaged, with a vastly expanded economy, and with the only margin of financial reserves available anywhere to get recovery and trade moving again—without the application of totalitarian methods. Yet we were destined, even then, not to remain the sole center of world power. The Soviet Union used totalitarian methods to force through an impressive economic recovery. And in the non-Communist world, we soon helped others to move in and share with us the world of power and influence. Western Europe had the will and the human talent to come through with a recovery more successful, more astonishing, and more impressive than the Soviet effort, because it was accomplished in a democratic framework. (And if we helped with our Marshall Plan, we should also remember that even in its peak year, the Marshall Plan provided only 4 percent of the resources to make that European recovery possible.) For a short time Europe might well have caught pneumonia if America sneezed. America did not sneeze, but neither are we completely reconciled to the fact that today nobody has all the antibodies.

The miracle of Japanese recovery and boom is only gradually dawning on us now. Beyond the world's industrial north, the classical colonial system came apart at the seams, with a further dispersion of political influence to new nations and new leaders who expect to have more than a little to say about how the world should be run.

We have not quite recovered, I think, from the feeling that somehow we have lost our grip on the world, because we are still living with the illusion that there was a time when almost everybody had to be agreeable with American ideas because almost everybody in the non-Communist world was dependent on American views.

A further source of frustration about world affairs is this: We forget too easily that this pluralistic world, full of ornery, independent people, is just what we have been working for and investing in and building a military shield to protect. We forget this because we are not used to the frustrating paradox that every time a major problem is solved, it creates a host of new problems; when we succeed in a major objective, we usually make so much new trouble that we forget to celebrate the successes just past. We labored hard to help Europe become strong and unified. But instead of dancing in the streets, there are those among us who complain today that the Europeans compete with us too hard, express too many independent ideas, and talk for all the world as if the grace of God had been shed on them also.

Or take the liberation of almost a billion people from the old colonial system—a process which we mightily helped to start and have cheered on ever since. The doctrine of self-determination—our doctrine—has carried the day. But instead of lighting bonfires on the hilltops, there are those among us who cannot get used to these uppity young nations which now insist on being equal and which act as though they were sovereign and independent. We squirm when we realize there is no alternative to helping them with the tricky new business of cranking up their economies and building up their governments along the general lines which we have always proclaimed to be the real "wave of the future." It is a very annoying habit—this tendency of each national success to give birth to a new set of national problems.

There is yet a fourth source of frustration: The nuclear age has imposed on great nations the most severe restraints on the exercise of military power. Time was when a big power could seriously think that a war might settle a disputed matter. Time was when a two-bit dictator did not go around thumbing his nose at a big power—it was considered unhealthy. But today, of course, the little war too easily becomes the big war; the big war too readily becomes nuclear war. So the price of power today is a teeth-clenching restraint and an extreme self-discipline.

## *Learning To Live with the Frustrations*

Yet we are learning to live with the frustrations of great power and of national success. Two events of this season are worth celebrating because they give evidence that we really are learning.

One of these events is the action of Congress in passing President Kennedy's new trade bill by a margin so lopsided that it is clear there is now an American consensus on this, one of the oldest debate topics in American political history. Americans know instinctively that we must go into partnership with Europe in freeing up world trade for the richer countries and the poorer countries alike.

The other event of the season is again summarized in a congressional vote. For the first time in its seventeen years, the United Nations received the full treatment this year as an issue in American domestic politics. The dramatic events in the Congo and the U.N. involvement in them sparked a special political interest when Congress, and the people at large through polls and letters to Washington, had to decide whether to buy $100 million worth of U.N. bonds.

For awhile, the Congress was inundated with anti-U.N. mail, and it did not look good. Not all political leaders are prepared to say, as a Senator told me at the time, "If I voted my mail, I'd *always* vote wrong." So those of us who were concerned with the fate of the U.N. loan were feeling a little like the man who called up the police station at Virginia Beach during the big storm last year, and said, "Come immediately. I am in dire circumstances. I am standing in two inches of water." The policeman said, "That is not enough to get excited about." And the man replied, "Yes, but I didn't tell you the whole story: I'm on the second floor already."

The organized good sense of the American community responded to this first real "crisis of confidence" over United States policy in the United Nations. In the end, what was proved—again—was what must be proved again and again each year: that our efforts to build an operational peace system through the United Nations are endorsed by the leadership and by most of the rank and file of both our great political parties. As we head now into another political campaign season, the recent reaffirmation by the Congress of bipartisanship in U.N. affairs is well worth noting in our national diary.

It was a cliff-hanger, though, at times. After all the turbulent talk about the U.N. in Congress, the overwhelming pro-U.N. vote came to many as a surprise—like the answer little Johnny got when he wrote a note to the girl sitting next to him in school, a typical masculine note: "Dear Mary, I love you. Do you love me? [Signed] Johnny." As Leo Rosten tells it, Johnny got back a lovely feminine note: "Dear Johnny, I do *not* [underlined three times] love you. Love, Mary."

Thus after the public debate appropriate to so important a matter, the Senate, by a vote of more than 3 to 1 (70–22), and the House of Representatives, by a vote of about 2 to 1 (256–134), responded to a deep conviction widely shared by most Americans: that the United Nations is never perfect, often frustrating, but always essential.

## Education for Understanding in International Affairs

It is the business of American education to take up the slack between our history of isolation and the new reality of our deep involvement in the frustrating and fascinating business of world politics. Since I transferred out of your world to help play this game from day to day, I no longer have to answer the most difficult question of seeing that educational values and national purposes serve each other. But I can tell you this: unless our educational system digs up the roots of American frustration about foreign affairs and plants instead the healthy seeds of American confidence, nothing we are doing in Washington can measure up to the enormous responsibilities which, in a democracy, the whole of the people must share with the President.

Educators can help by teaching about events past and current—not from the critics' standpoint, but from the point of view of the people who had the responsibility for shaping them. If we understand how complex was the brooding of a Lincoln or a Wilson, we can begin to visualize the burden we place on a modern President.

If our students can learn that we never lost our all-powerful grip on the world because we never had it, or wanted it, maybe they will be better able to live in a world with many centers of power. If each new generation of Americans comes to understand that, as a matter of course, the "solution" of each problem creates several more problems to worry about, perhaps they will be less prone than their parents to snatch a psychic defeat from the jaws of each new victory. If the explosive curve of modern science and technology is required knowledge for every student, perhaps in time every adult will better understand why the many restraints on the use of great power have little to do with timidity or treason but much to do with science and technology.

And if every student can learn, when it comes to public affairs, to play the "Let's Pretend" game, putting himself in the place of the man who has to make the decisions, perhaps more Americans in the future than in the past will understand how many and various are the ingredients of a political judgment and how wondrous are the fascinations of public responsibility.

There is hardly an issue in world affairs worth discussing which is not interrelated with other issues; which does not involve a mix of strategic, political, economic, and other factors; which does not involve elements which we control and elements which we do not control; which does not involve contradictions between domestic politics and international politics—for ourselves and for everyone else party to the issue. Policies and actions in world affairs therefore must be relevant to complex and shifting situations at precise moments in time; abstractions alone are no good, and simplifications can be fatal.

So, I would settle for this: All Americans should be taught at every stage of their education that, in matters of American foreign policy, we are closer to the truth when we magnify the complexity of it all, and furthest from the truth when we oversimplify to get an easy answer.

# THE CARNEGIE STUDY
# OF THE FEDERAL GOVERNMENT
# AND HIGHER EDUCATION

### Nathan M. Pusey
PRESIDENT, HARVARD UNIVERSITY

THE CARNEGIE STUDY OF THE FEDERAL GOVERNMENT AND HIGHER EDUCA-
tion was set up in 1959 to shed light on the new relationship—
now widely recognized to be of extraordinary significance—which has
developed during the past twenty years between various agencies of
the Government and our colleges and universities. The Study, conducted by a staff of two, was guided by an advisory committee of
university presidents, all of them trustees of the Carnegie Foundation
for the Advancement of Teaching. It was supported by a grant from
the Carnegie Corporation. Its results—based on self-studies of their
operations during the academic year 1959–60 conducted by twenty-six
cooperating institutions of higher education—are to be published by
the American Council on Education. This Study also makes extensive
use of information gathered by the staff to illuminate practices and
points of view of the many Government agencies involved in the new
association.

The report of the Study first discusses what has, so far, been for the
universities the most significant source of Federal funds—project
research sponsored by the Government. The practice of making
grants and contracts for research with individual scientists was begun
by the Government during the war years to mobilize science in the
academic community for the war effort. It has grown steadily ever
since, until today various agencies of the Federal Government spend
hundreds of millions of dollars each year in institutions of higher
learning through this instrumentality. The nation seems fully conscious
of the value of scientific research, and Federal expenditures for this
purpose encounter no serious public opposition.

17

## Institutions in the Study

The twenty-six institutions, whose experiences with the Federal Government form the substratum of the Carnegie Study, were chosen to be fairly representative, in size, kind, and location, of the spectrum of higher education in this country. Together they received 28 percent of all Government money spent in institutions of higher learning for project research in 1959–60. They fall into four main categories.

The first category of twelve universities, public and private, is made up of institutions with large commitments to research. Most of these have a broad range of strong graduate schools. They are: University of California at Berkeley, at Los Angeles, and at San Diego; California Institute of Technology, University of Chicago, Cornell University, Harvard University, Massachusetts Institute of Technology, University of Michigan, Princeton University, Stanford University, and University of Texas. The amount of Federal money spent in each of these institutions for project research in the academic year 1959–60 ranged from a low of $5 million at the California Institute of Technology to $20 million at the University of Michigan.

These are large amounts, but their magnitude should occasion no surprise in view of the now widely recognized fact that more than 95 percent of Federal support for research in two thousand institutions of higher learning goes to fewer than one hundred such institutions. At the same time, it is necessary to remember that the more than $1 billion spent by the Federal Government for research and development in colleges and universities—including the amounts spent in support of a number of very large off-campus laboratories under university management—is only a small fraction (less than 10 percent) of the full amount allotted by the Government for research and development. It is also important to remember that the large majority of colleges—and the fields of the social sciences and humanities in all institutions—have felt almost no impact from Federal research programs.

The second category of institutions in the Study is composed of six universities, each of which received from $1.5 million to $3.5 million Federal money for project research during 1959–60. These are: University of California at Davis, Indiana University, Iowa State University, Pennsylvania State University, Syracuse University, and

Tulane University. Four institutions make up the Study's third category. They are: University of Louisville, University of Notre Dame, Union University (New York), and University of Wyoming, each of which received from $100,000 to $1.5 million. The four institutions of the final category—a teachers college (Arkansas State Teachers College), two liberal arts colleges (Catawba College and Lawrence College), and a public engineering college (Newark College of Engineering)—were relatively uninvolved in Federal programs. Newark received $24,000; two of the others received nothing in support.

## Purpose, Source, and Amounts of Federal Funds

Project grant funds undergirded an indescribable range and variety of research activity in the institutions involved, though in every case only in limited areas within them. Much of the total was spent in medical and dental schools and in schools of public health. Virtually all the rest went to engineering and agricultural schools, or to departments of biology, astronomy, mathematics, chemistry, physics, and others of the natural sciences, and to psychology. Schools of law, business, and public administration, other graduate and professional schools, as well as colleges and divisions of arts and letters, were almost untouched by this very large flow of Federal money. It is hard to see how the situation could have been otherwise, since thus far considerations of health, defense, economic development, and the need for scientific advance alone have had the power to release such funds. A third of the Federal dollars going to Stanford and Princeton, 50 percent of M.I.T.'s and 70 percent of Michigan's were spent for research in engineering, while 54 percent of Harvard's, 67 percent of Louisville's, and 93 percent of Union's were spent in the medical area.

Twenty-eight different agencies of the Government were listed as sponsors of at least one program in one or another of the twenty-six institutions of the Carnegie Study. On the other hand, most of the $130.4 million in project research money going to these institutions came from a relatively small number of agencies. The National Institutes of Health and the Department of Defense supplied the largest amounts. Following them—though at some remove—came the National Science Foundation, the Atomic Energy Commission, the Department of Agriculture, and more recently—important only beyond the term of the Study, but coming up fast—the National Aeronautics and Space Administration.

Looking for the moment only at the underwriting of project research in the institutions themselves in the year 1959–60, the Department of Defense was the source of 70 percent of the support Michigan received from the Federal Government that year, 78 percent of San Diego's, 66 percent of Princeton's, 62 percent of Stanford's, and 56 percent of Texas'; while the National Institutes of Health provided 53 percent of the support which came to Harvard, 72 percent of Tulane's, and 81 percent of Louisville's.

Some of the institutions participating in the Carnegie Study are, as I have mentioned, further involved with Government as managers, alone or with others, of separate laboratories set up to conduct programs of research, much of it often requiring an interdisciplinary approach. The need for programs in laboratories of this kind was recognized early in the war years when it was already evident—not least because of developments in the nuclear field—that the approach through individual project grants, however numerous, could not possibly meet the full range of requirements for scientific advance. Occasionally these "separate" laboratories are both on a university campus and are intimately connected with the staple work going on there. In other instances they are at some remove, and their activity is only distantly related to the sponsoring institution's central endeavor. Sometimes they provide opportunity for training graduate students; sometimes they do not. Occasionally they are managed by associations of universities; in at least one instance—though its facilities are made available to university scientists—an industrial corporation furnishes the management.

Among them are such scientific establishments as the National Laboratories of the Atomic Energy Commission—Brookhaven, managed by the Associated Universities; Argonne, by the University of Chicago; Los Alamos, by the University of California; and Oak Ridge by the Union Carbide Nuclear Company. But there are many others, most of which are listed in the Carnegie Study as "separate research facilities."

Though the annual budgets of some of these operations are relatively small (say from $1 million to $5 million), a few statistics will suggest the considerable magnitude of some of the others. Most impressive perhaps is the $96 million spent during 1959–60 at the Lawrence Radiation Laboratory associated with the University of California (the sum would have been $122 million if construction costs had been included). This amount was more than two times the $45 million spent in the same period on the Berkeley campus of the University of California for all other operating expenses for educational and general purposes. Similarly, the $53 million expense of operating its Jet Propulsion Laboratory in 1959–60 was almost five times the amount spent by the California Institute of Technology for its own general and educational expenses that year ($11,685,000). And the operating expenses of M.I.T.'s Lincoln Laboratory ($34 million) almost equaled the $37 million spent by that institution on its campus proper for educational and general purposes during the same period.

Measured in dollars, support for research and development, either in the institutions themselves or in laboratories affiliated with them, now running at an annual rate of well over $1 billion, easily provides the main avenue by which Federal funds now come into educational institutions. But there are other significant, if lesser, byways through which Federal funds come to institutions of higher learning.

Important sums are made available as fellowships and loans, and as research assistantships, to help students further their work, and in other forms to reimburse faculty people for consulting and investigative activities, though programs providing these kinds of help are relatively small in size. In only four cases in the Carnegie Study did they exceed $1 million.

Undergraduates are aided by several programs in addition to those for veterans, such as the new summer assistantship program of the National Science Foundation, and the loan program of the National Defense Education Act. But graduate fellowship programs are more typical of Government assistance to students. Such aid, coming from a number of agencies, totaled 17,000 Federal fellowships last year. It is perhaps inevitable that these fellowships should tend to be concentrated in the relatively small number of institutions with the strongest graduate programs.

Even more important than fellowships is the support that comes to graduate students—again very largely graduate students in the sciences—through research assistantships. The number of such assistantships has increased vastly. Though the full amount of this kind of help now being furnished to scientists is unknown, perhaps its extent can be imagined from a fact reported by the Division of Research of the Atomic Energy Commission: in December 1961 there were 2,185 graduate students working as research assistants along with 2,173 senior scientists on research projects supported in institutions of higher learning—this by 528 contracts involving total costs of $54.8 million. It is estimated that perhaps as many as 25,000 graduate students are now being helped by research assistantships each year. More significant perhaps for those especially concerned for the advance of science in this country is the further estimate that as many as 90 percent of graduate students in the sciences are dependent on Federal funds for support sometime during the period of their graduate training.

A complete account of the present involvement of the Federal Government and universities would include an analysis of the many services, including consulting, which people in universities perform for agencies of Government, and would thus make clear that this is not a one-way traffic situation. For example, most of the 1,700 scientists listed in 1960 as members of the advisory groups of the Public Health Service were university people. It is impossible even to guess the full extent of this kind of service performed by university people for agencies of the Federal Government, but it took more than twenty pages in Harvard's self-study simply to list the agencies and the departments of the University which are linked with them. And Harvard's financial officers estimate it cost the University $200,000 to pay the fringe benefits and salaries of faculty members retained as consultants by Federal agencies in 1959–60.

The Federal agencies with the largest appropriations to allocate to research and development are those responsible for defense, health, and science. Since it is chiefly the impact of these agencies that the universities have been experiencing, there is perhaps no ground for expecting the Government to have shown concern for education or for the educational institutions themselves. And yet through Federal programs now existing much has been done directly, and even more indirectly, toward these ends. Let me quickly remind you of a few instances.

The Federal Government has been making appropriations to the land-grant colleges for a hundred years. The appropriations to these institutions for 1962, exclusive of all funds coming to them from research grants and the like, totaled more than $100 million. A policy of distributing Federal surplus property, both personal and real, to institutions of higher education was adopted immediately following World War II and has been of great value. The Housing Act of 1950 set up a College Housing Loan Program. By the 1960's more than 40 percent of all new dormitories and other revenue-producing structures on college campuses were being constructed under this or succeeding legislation. By 1963 the amount of these loans will exceed $2 billion, and though not all institutions have been willing to participate, more than a thousand have, with the result that housing has been provided for more than a quarter million students.

The Hill-Burton Act has helped finance hospitals and health facilities. The National Institutes of Health, the National Science Foundation, the Atomic Energy Commission, and the Department of Defense have all built laboratories. A bill before the Eighty-seventh Congress would have provided $1.5 billion for libraries, laboratories, and other non-revenue-producing properties to help forward the advance of science; but you all know its—at least temporary—sorry fate.

Fortunately there are indications of growing understanding. Agencies are beginning to look beyond supporting single scientists pursuing particular experiments and are showing concern for larger institutional programs of research, including programs in which a number of scientists from different disciplines may be involved, and programs requiring large and costly laboratories and instrumentation. The National Institutes of Health are now allocating 5 percent of their project research budget to "general research support grants." The percentage will grow by stages to 15 percent. Similarly, the National Science Foundation is now providing for what it calls "institutional grants" (a percentage of its grants and contracts in a particular institution up to a maximum of $50,000 which the institution is free to spend as it wishes for the advancement of science on its premises). And, though the Constitution says nothing about a Federal responsibility for education, there are already other programs in operation or in prospect which exhibit both a recognition of the importance of the health of the institution itself and a willingness to give the institution more to say about how its research funds should be spent.

Nor have agencies of the Federal Government been completely unconcerned for the curricular and instructional components of education. The National Science Foundation and the Office of Education have sponsored the revision of basic texts in chemistry, physics, mathematics, biology, various foreign languages, English, and anthropology. Much support to strengthen instruction has been provided for members of faculties, and as indicated earlier, for students, especially graduate and postdoctoral students, and among these especially for students in the sciences. It is perhaps pertinent to note that 60 percent of the graduate and 25 percent of the undergraduate, or 52 percent of all the students of public health are now federally sponsored. And it is conservatively estimated that by 1970 the Federal Government will be providing 40 percent of the operating costs of the nation's medical schools as well as 80 percent of their outlays for research.

Title VI of the National Defense Education Act of 1958—a law brought into being out of concern for our country's ability to get on in a world grown perilously small—authorized the establishment of language and area centers. The Fulbright Act, the Smith-Mundt Act, and the Fulbright-Hays Act have sustained an expensive program of faculty and student exchanges between the United States and other nations. Some 50,000 exchanges have thus far been sponsored by these programs. And there are other programs under the auspices of agencies like AID, ICA, and the Peace Corps, which together have done much to strengthen concern for world affairs in colleges and universities.

Let me say in summary that in fiscal 1960, agencies of the Federal Government spent about a billion dollars in institutions of higher education—$450 million for research, $44 million for facilities, $388 million for scholarships and fellowships, and $217 million for various programs of instruction. The large total does not include the amounts spent in separate laboratories, or other amounts provided for loans and in the distribution of surplus property. Were these added, the figure would be almost doubled.

Thus, it is clear that income from the Federal Government has already come to play a large role in the finances of universities. Along with income from tuition, state appropriations, gifts, and income from endowment, it is now not only a source of support for research but also a major source of operating revenue, especially for some institutions with strong programs of graduate study. All this and more is made quite clear in the self-studies which underlie the Carnegie Study.

## Problems and Responsibilities Imposed by Federal Funds

Without exception, the heads of the twenty-six institutions participating in the Study said that their involvement with the Federal Government has proved to be a "good thing." Good, because it has stimulated research (there can be no question but that the great scientific advance in America during the past twenty years could never have happened without these large Federal funds); good, because programs of the various agencies of the Federal Government have provided expensive laboratories, buildings, and research facilities the universities could never have acquired with their own means; good, because of the support and encouragement that have come to professors and graduate students. Federal funds have played an enormously important role during the past two decades in fostering research, and in instituting, extending, diversifying, and enriching programs of graduate study. This represents a wholly praiseworthy achievement. And yet, at the same time, there is another side to the story.

To begin with, there is the very large increase in administrative work required by doing such huge business with the Federal Government. Especially vexing are the frequent and formidable demands made on the time of valuable research professors to prepare applications for support, to administer the funds allocated, and to make elaborate reports on the uses to which the funds have been put. Large Federal funds have a way of turning scientists into administrative officers. There are numerous other particular points of difficulty, such as questions concerning transfers of title to equipment and uncertainty whether the Bureau of Internal Revenue will construe various awards to individuals as fellowship funds or as salary. Science advances, yes; but red tape advances too!

But easily the most onerous and vexing difficulties brought about by these large increments of Federal support are those occasioned by the fact that certain of the agencies have adamantly refused to pay the full cost of the research they sponsor in universities. A college or university accepts a grant or a contract because a member of its faculty needs the support to get on with his work, because his work is important for his growth as a scholar and contributes to the advance of knowledge, and also because the work fits a Federal agency's conception of its role in the national purpose. For all these reasons, the college or university agrees to accept support from an agency of Government only to find that the institution is then caught up in the necessity of adding funds of its own to make possible the furtherance of this agency's mission.

It is easy to say the college or university does not need to do this. Obviously at one level this is true; but not if you take into consideration the need to advance science, and the present pressing need to develop scientists in the national interest.

This a point of major difficulty. One of the institutions in the Carnegie Study which is contributing $179,000 annually of its own funds to supplement Federal support of research activities in its department of biology reports that it has no money to establish a department of psychology. Another major institution has no funds for a new library building it has needed—one could say without much exaggeration, has desperately needed—for years. And yet this institution is expending sums to supplement its inadequately reimbursed research grants which, could they be put aside, would pay for a new library in five years. There are other examples of the same thing.

Though inadequately reimbursed costs provide perhaps the sorest point in the whole relationship, there are additional grounds for unhappiness. A similar pressure is exerted on an institution's free funds by programs to provide research space and facilities which require matching funds. Increasing sums being made available to support research constantly invite more applications, lead to more awards, and eventuate in steadily increasing demands within an institution for more space and more facilities. And this is not all.

Federal funds are made available only to some departments within a college or university and for research only in the limited number of areas of inquiry which happen to be of interest to this or that agency of Government with a definite and specific mission of its own to perform. So pressures are set up which could easily effect imbalances within and among departments. It is not inconceivable that the presence of large sums of money in this or that area can exert a shaping influence on faculty research programs or cause graduate students to move into well-supported areas of investigation. Some have begun to fear lest a faculty have less to say about the focus of its research effort than it should. Not that its members will have no power to resist blandishments, but that the choice with which they will be confronted will be to do research in a particular area or not to do it at all.

Another question concerns the distorting influence these enormous funds may have in turning a professor's loyalty from his department and institution to his own laboratory and to the research area of his interest—not necessarily to be construed as a bad thing. But the basic worry underlying all these considerations is real, namely, that while the investigator will continue in theory to have complete freedom of choice about what he will study, in fact his freedom of choice will be confined within those areas of investigation where agencies of Government for their own reasons have chosen to make money available. No one can say whether this is a real or only a fancied danger at the moment—or if it exists, how serious the danger is— but it seems obvious that, over a period of years, in their power to grant or withhold funds, the agencies of Government are likely to have much to say about the direction research is to follow, whereas many educational leaders continue to believe this kind of decision had best be left to the colleges and universities themselves.

A related difficulty is that the encouragement of research within a university will make it increasingly difficult for a faculty to show proper concern for instruction of undergraduates. Again, it is too early to say this has happened, but there is widespread fear that it may happen. And there are other concerns of related kind.

## Questions Posed by the Carnegie Study

In the end, therefore, the Carnegie Study concludes with a series of questions:

Basically and most important, will the new and growing association with Government strengthen or weaken our educational institutions in their ability to perform their essential work? The answer to this question will be found only in a multiplicity of responses given over a long period of time to a host of related, more pointed queries. Will future Government regulatory policies adequately recognize the true nature of educational institutions? Or will they simply treat our colleges and universities as service agencies in particular situations?

Will Government recognize that education is as properly a matter for national concern as are defense, health, technical, and economic advance? Will the Government's programs make proper allowance for basic as well as for applied research? And for teaching? Will Government recognize how important it is that an institution of higher learning strive to advance simultaneously and consistently along a broad front of academic interests rather than be content to make occasional spurts ahead in some limited area of immediate concern? Will leaders of Government actively support, not merely pay lip service to, the idea that the social studies and the humanities are also relevant in considerations of national strength?

A further serious matter: Will programs of the Government affecting higher education show proper care not to weaken the bastions against political interference which educational leaders have been slowly building through centuries? Will they recognize that to realize its purpose a college or university must have the final say over the nature and direction of its educational and investigative activities?

Will Government programs be adequately sensitive to the fact that good education and good research require steadfast concern for standards of excellence, and that neither will be achieved if it becomes a guiding aim of Government programs to keep everyone happy and to avoid hard choices? From the other side, will colleges and universities recognize that they have to change to meet new needs? Will they organize themselves to work cooperatively with agencies of Government, ceasing to go their own ways and to contend selfishly among themselves? Will they also concede that they have an obligation to work with Government, not only to advance knowledge but also to extend educational opportunity? More particularly, will representatives of the institutions of higher education find effective ways to sit down with informed and concerned representatives from Government to evolve wise policies, and then—even more important— to get them understood in the Congress and in the country at large?

## Conclusion

A new, complicated, imperfect, but incalculably significant—and promising—relationship between the Federal Government and institutions of higher learning has grown up during the past two decades almost without direction. The overreaching question it now raises for us all is how to work together in the years immediately ahead to perfect this relationship in both education's and the nation's interest. Can we, for example, in this next period find some more considerable middle ground between the present largely mission-oriented Federal programs on the one hand and an unwanted and dangerous program of general Federal support for higher education on the other? This is the big question which must be answered in a multitude of smaller decisions.

Finally, let me say that if any conclusion emerges from the Carnegie Study it is perhaps that we must all disenthrall our minds from old attitudes and narrow interests—we in education and they in Government—and mutually recognize that we now share a joint responsibility to advance knowledge on a world-wide stage. If we are to discharge this task, we must learn to work together to minimize the incoherencies which now exist on both sides of the relationship, and move on to forge a constructive alliance which, not least because it will be established in self-interest on both sides—will truly serve the nation's interest.

It is the conviction of all who participated in the Carnegie Study that the sound choices needed to develop and perfect the new relationship are not beyond the wisdom of congressmen, agency administrators, and educators, if only we can learn to work together and will set our minds resolutely to the task.

# STUDENT AID
# AND THE FEDERAL GOVERNMENT

## Rexford G. Moon, Jr.
DIRECTOR, COLLEGE SCHOLARSHIP SERVICE,
COLLEGE ENTRANCE EXAMINATION BOARD

A NYONE WHO HAS EVER UNDERTAKEN A STUDY OF FEDERAL GOVERN-
ment expenditures, whether for aid to education or for crop allot-
ments, will detect a familiar ring in statements such as:

I am sure you will understand there are many different programs at various
levels managed and paid for in different ways by many agencies in which
this Bureau receives benefits. Unfortunately, the necessary research work
and the scope of the problem involved to furnish you complete and accurate
information in these areas is beyond . . .[1]

or

the total cost of the programs described . . . cannot be determined in any
precise way.[2]

or

The breakdown of program data on the basis of fields of study, academic
levels, and kinds of recipients is difficult in many programs. Records are
usually not kept for reporting on this basis.[3]

These statements and others like them were my introduction to a
quest started about a year ago for facts and figures on Federal activities related to student financial aid. This search was part of a larger
study of all student aid activities in the United States which I had

[1] Communication from the Department of the Navy to the author, Sept. 15,
1961.

[2] U.S. House of Representatives, Committee on Government Operations, *Government Programs in International Education (A Survey and Handbook)*. 85th
Cong., 2d Sess. (Washington: Government Printing Office, 1959).

[3] Penrose B. Jackson and Dolores A. Steinhilber, *Federal Funds for Education:
Fields, Levels, Recipients, 1959 and 1960*, Office of Education Circular 679
(Washington: Government Printing Office, 1962).

undertaken for Dr. Frank H. Bowles and Unesco. It is from this study that much of the data for this paper was taken.[4]

These statements served as a constant reminder that attempting to decipher this phase of Federal aid to education is not unlike trying to chart an iceberg-infested ocean. One sees many things, but realizes from experience and advance information that there may be much more below the surface than on top. One also learns quickly that icebergs are always on the move, that their shapes are always changing, and—perhaps most relevant for this discussion—that new ones are forming faster than old ones are melting away. Though these quotes and this simile may provide amusement, their purpose is to serve as caveats for certain of the facts and figures which follow.

In order to assure reasonable consistency across areas, agencies, and programs, only those Federal Government programs have been included in this analysis which: (1) actually provide some type of financial payment to the individual to relieve him of some or all of the educational and/or personal costs connected with study at some level of higher education; *and* (2) are conducted or become available at a higher institution (not operated by the Government) or at a center administered by such an institution, and/or (3) require the individual to pursue a course of study and/or research which is, or is similar to, what he might pursue as a full-time student working for an undergraduate or graduate degree.

Intradepartmental, on-the-job training programs are excluded except where the evidence is clear that they are offered in a university; also excluded are programs offered in Government schools, prisons, or other "higher institutions." The dollar figures indicated for various programs represent only funds paid to or credited to *individuals*. In some instances these are estimates, since a fair number of programs do not report expenditures in this way.

One other point of qualification. There are now probably over 300 educational or training programs supported by the Federal Government, many of which have student financial aid implications.[5] Of these,

[4] Rexford G. Moon, Jr., *Student Financial Assistance in the United States, Administration and Resources* (New York: College Entrance Examination Board, 1963).

[5] U.S. House of Representatives, Committee on Education and Labor, *A Directory of Federally Financed Student Loans, Fellowships and Career Training Programs in the Field of Higher Education*, 87th Cong., 2d Sess. (Washington: Government Printing Office, 1962).

those that are small, fall outside our definition, defy classification, or for which information is lacking have been excluded from this analysis. Of the approximately 300 programs, there are about 30 major ones, and it is with these that this paper deals.

Federal programs intended primarily to provide financial assistance to individuals have only a thirty-year tradition. However, higher institutions' concern for the effects of educational costs upon able but impecunious students is as old as the institutions. Jefferson said that scholarships were necessary in order "to avail the commonwealth of those talents and virtues which nature has sown as liberally among the poor as among the rich . . ." But often these "charity funds" for "charity students" became, by virtue of their name, self-defeating in the face of the Jacksonian mood of the 1850's. Eventually the egalitarian will triumphed and the term "scholarship" replaced the term "charity," but, as Rudolph notes, this was "a substitution that took place without any change in actual meaning, for scholarship meant 'needy' long before it also meant qualified by scholarly excellence." [6] If we judge efforts to provide higher education at little or no cost to the individual as a student aid effort, the Land-Grant Act of a hundred years ago may be considered the first Federal student aid program since "engraved in the land-grant idea was the concept of collegiate education for everyone at public expense." [7] Some states had started student aid programs before 1900.

It is, however, a big jump from 1862 to 1933—the point at which the first formal Federal program of direct student support emerged. Administered by the National Youth Administration, it provided funds by which institutions might support student work programs. The real reasons for this program are obscured by time. Some say its purpose was to help college students continue their education; others, that it was to keep students off the labor market during those bad times. It apparently accomplished at least some of both purposes, for during the period 1935–43, over 600,000 students benefited from these funds.[8] The big question, then and now, was in what kind of jobs. Critics contended that all the program accomplished was to support busy

[6] Frederick Rudolph, *The American College and University: A History* (New York: Alfred A. Knopf, 1962).

[7] *Ibid.*

[8] Alice Rivlin, *The Role of the Federal Government in Financing Higher Education* (Washington: Brookings Institution, 1961).

work on the campuses. Even the first Federal student aid program was apparently not without its critics.

World War II saw the first Federal student loan program, in which juniors and seniors or graduate and professional students in science, engineering, or health programs could borrow up to $500 per year if they agreed to work in the war effort after graduation. (Federal loans with various strings attached apparently came into being before 1958!) During the two years of its operation (1943 and 1944), about 11,000 students borrowed a total of $3 million.[9] One more point of history: 1944 produced the Servicemen's Readjustment Act, or GI bill, and its companion for disabled veterans, Public Law 16, Seventy-eighth Congress. The programs thus created were student aid programs in every sense of the word. The GI bill, in one sense, anyway, represented reaffirmation of the implied, if not stated, land-grant concept of the availability of free higher education for all at public expense, but this time not necessarily only in public institutions. By 1944, jobs, loans, and efforts, both direct and indirect, to provide free higher education, first through land grants and then through "people grants," had emerged as Federal methods of student support. These aid forms have been often repeated in other Federal student support programs since that time.

Since 1944 there has been, as we know, a tremendous growth in Federal programs related to, and/or in support of, higher education. To recount all the developments of the last twenty years and their student aid implications would take too much time. Like our icebergs, most of them are still with us in some shape or form and can be reported. Where we are now is of greatest interest; therefore, I propose to jump immediately into the present, or at least as close to the present as is permitted by the published or otherwise available data about Federal efforts. In most instances, this will not be later than 1960 or 1961.

The totality of Federal support of, and activities in connection with, higher education may, according to the Council's Annual Meeting program, be subdivided into five broad categories: loans and grants for capital improvements; research programs; programs of education and training; programs of international education; and programs of student financial assistance.[10] Aid in some form or other to students is

[9] Ibid.
[10] American Council on Education, Program of the Forty-fifth Annual Meeting, October 3–5, 1962.

part of many of the major Federal programs in each of these support areas. In order to do justice, then, to the pervasiveness of Federal student aid efforts, I am going to use this rubric to describe the welter of federally sponsored programs. With the exception of the area of loans and grants for capital improvements, the other major areas of Federal activity or involvement support one or more programs of a student aid nature.

In 1960, the Federal Government spent approximately $770,403,-000 [11] in support of its various special programs at the level of higher education and an additional $800 million [12] for research in colleges and universities, of which about half was for general grants and contracts and half for the maintenance of government-owned research centers managed by institutions of higher learning. Of this total of $1,570,403,000, I estimate that $366,540,000, or 23 percent of the total was devoted in some form or other—intended, implied, or permitted—to the direct assistance of individuals with the expenses of some type of higher education. If we parcel out federally sponsored research, the student aid implications of which I shall discuss next, the total dollar value of direct support of students by the nonresearch programs of Government rises to over 40 percent of the total. From the evidence at hand, no one could say, without contradicting the obvious, that the support of individuals with the direct or indirect expenses of their education was a minor or improper activity of the Federal Government.

## Programs of Research

The Federal Government's dollar support of research activities in colleges and universities is over half the total Federal expenditure for higher educational purposes. These monies, quite inadvertently, support one of the largest covert programs of student aid maintained by Federal funds. It has been estimated that at the present time perhaps as many as 40,000 students,[13] most of them at the graduate level,

[11] Jackson and Steinhilber, *op. cit.*

[12] J. Kenneth Little, *A Survey of Federal Programs in Higher Education—Summary*, Office of Education Bulletin 1963, No. 5 (Washington: Government Printing Office, 1962).

[13] Executive Office of the President, Bureau of the Budget, *Special Analysis of Federal Research and Development Programs in the 1962 Budget* (Washington: Government Printing Office, 1961).

receive assistance with maintenance and/or educational expenses as a direct result of the availability of these funds in institutions of higher education. If we estimate, as one author has, that, based on 1954 figures, each individual receives on an average $1,600 per year,[14] the funds used for student aid from this source alone would quite conservatively be estimated to be $64 million per year. However, in view of current student support practices, this figure is probably too conservative. It is more likely that the expenditure for this purpose now averages $2,000 per student, or in toto as much as $80 million per year.

Since 91 percent of the funds for research come from the Department of Defense, the Public Health Service, NSF, AEC, and NASA,[15] one must conclude that graduate science education is aided almost exclusively. Here again is the familiar problem of the concentration of Federal funds in a few institutions. This concentration puts in the hands of just a few institutions great power for the recruitment of graduate students and for the expansion of graduate programs in the sciences.

There has been much talk and even some formal efforts in and out of Government to balance the lopsidedness of the support of graduate education in the sciences. But as these numbers indicate, the problem of achieving balance is one of considerable magnitude. These figures show how large the expenditure would have to be to neutralize the impact of federally supported research, let alone the impact of the concentration in science of expenditures of industry and those of other programs of Government. Suffice it to say that this activity exists and persists. Little is known about it in detail, yet it may be one of the most influential in shaping the strength and image of graduate education in our major institutions. It deserves to be explored in greater depth and soon.

## Programs of Education and Training

A second broad area of Federal activity which depends heavily upon higher education for services, and thereby provides income to institutions and secondarily to individuals, relates to the broad areas

[14] Rivlin, *op. cit.*
[15] *Ibid.*

covered by programs of education and training supported by the Federal Government.

Generally speaking, the purposes of these programs are to "increase the quality of highly trained manpower in specified fields, to increase the competency of the sponsoring agencies' employees or to raise the capabilities of educational institutions and programs in specified fields." [16] In most instances, higher institutions receive funds from the Government for the operation and maintenance of certain courses or programs of study and from these funds the institutions reimburse participants in these programs for various expenses. In the main, these programs are "manpower orientated." Large numbers of individuals are aided each year in meeting a welter of expenses related to some type of specialized higher education. It could be said that in some instances the aid is provided as an inducement to the individual to seek specialized training or to reimburse him for a loss of salary or wages while in training.

The majority of individuals aided by these programs are not full-time students nor are they working toward a degree. The aid may come to the individual in many forms: remission of fees, subsistence allowances for self and dependents, allowances for travel, provision of study materials, and the like. In most instances, Federal regulations specify who shall receive what amount and type of assistance. For the most part, the duration of these programs is less than one year.

This is an area where considerable numbers of colleges are involved (according to Little, 450 in 1959 [17]), but also where it is very difficult to determine with much accuracy the number of individuals assisted or the total dollar expenditure on their behalf. The various programs may provide funds either to individuals to attend regular institutionally maintained educational programs, or to an institution to establish a special program, some portion of the funds for which may be used to aid individuals to participate in that program. The Federal agencies involved are many; graduate, undergraduate, and specialized education, all are supported.

In this category should be included the various summer and full-time institutes of the NSF for science and mathematics teachers,

[16] Little, *op. cit.*
[17] *Ibid.*

which in 1960 numbered 649 and aided 31,000 teachers to the extent of an estimated $24 million in stipends and allowances.[18] Also properly belonging here, according to our definitions, are all advanced ROTC programs, including the Holloway Plan, aiding in total about 27,000 undergraduates to the extent of $11,450,000 in 1960; the NDEA Guidance and Language Institutes, providing subsistence payments in 1960–61 of $6,366,000 to about 5,840 teachers; the various traineeship and training-grant programs of NIH, aiding 18,299 individuals with about $19,577,000 in various stipends; and the large program of the Department of Defense for its employees and military personnel, which aided about 41,000 persons to the extent of $11,553,000 in 1959–60.[19] This is the most amorphous of areas of Government support to students. Many different agencies are involved. Some persons may question whether it is even appropriate to include some or all of these programs in a discussion of financial aid to individuals. I would contend that it is. For who is to say that these programs are not in part really only compensatory for the failure to provide more extensive educational opportunities to individuals at the time of their original formal training.

There are many more programs than those mentioned which may properly belong in this category, including programs of the Office of Vocational Rehabilitation, Social Security Administration, AEC, Food and Drug Administration, USIA, Departments of Justice, Commerce, Interior, Agriculture, Labor, Treasury, Post Office, NASA, and others. However, many are small or defy classification so they have not been included. Certainly in any long-range examination of our educational programming in the United States, the question should be explored whether these activities are indicative of inadequacies in our continuing, full-time educational services or only reflect the rapidly changing nature of our national needs and the explosion of knowledge and thus are only temporary in nature. One could argue, I suppose, that adequate investments in full-time education could, over time, minimize the need for many of these programs since there is about them an unmistakable remedial quality. The figures herein reported for the major programs in this area represent a yearly investment in as many as 123,000 people of about $73 million.

[18] Moon, *op. cit.*
[19] *Ibid.*

## Programs of International Education

That the Federal Government plays a role in furthering the international exchange of persons is well known. It is, however, and this fact too may be well known, extremely difficult to obtain a clear indication of the numbers of persons involved and particularly, from the data available, of the amounts of money utilized for this purpose.

Two agencies in the Department of State account for the largest part of the Federal effort to aid individuals in international exchange. These are the Bureau of Educational and Cultural Affairs and the Agency for International Development (formerly ICA). There are, however, other agencies or departments involved in foreign exchange activities, such as NSF, AEC, Department of the Interior, Department of Defense, Department of Labor. The efforts of these other agencies are small and have not been included in this analysis.

According to the Institute of International Education, there were in 1960–61, 15,000 Americans studying abroad in contrast to 53,000 foreign nationals studying in this country. The Bureau of Educational and Cultural Affairs international exchange program provided, in 1959, aid to 5,532 foreign nationals and 2,231 Americans abroad at a cost of $26,590,482. In the same year it is reported [20] that AID (as ICA) assisted 6,211 foreign nationals to study or travel in this country and 1,934 persons to study or travel in countries other than the U.S. These efforts cost $24,996,000. ICA (now AID) also assisted in 1959, and presumably annually after that, about 600 students, both American and foreign, under its so-called university contract program.[21] Possibly as much as $18 million, or about $3,000 per student, was spent here. It would appear then that during 1960–61 at least 16,358 persons, American and foreign nationals, were assisted in exchange activities by the Federal Government to the extent of possibly as much as $49 million. How many of these individuals were actually following programs of study in higher institutions is difficult to determine. A recent report [22] indicates that "students" represented 46 percent of those aided by the Bureau's program in 1959. Assuming this same percentage

[20] U.S. House of Representatives, Committee on Education and Labor, *op. cit.*
[21] *Ibid.*
[22] Charles A. Quattlebaum, *Federal Educational Policies, Programs and Proposals,* Part III: *Analyses and Classification of Programs* (Washington: Government Printing Office, 1960).

applied to the total group, we would estimate that 7,525 students received as much as $22,540,000 in assistance in the year under review.

## Programs of Student Financial Assistance

Now we come to the last major area—that of student financial assistance from Federal sources. I have saved for discussion here those programs whose purpose is to make *full-time* college attendance in the United States possible for U.S. nationals. In this area, one finds many different types of aid. It is in this area that the Federal Government maintains its most extensive contacts with higher institutions. All but 400 of the approximately 2,000 higher institutions in the country participate in some way or another in one or more federally sponsored or supported student aid programs.[23] These programs provide aid to a variety of groups, including loans for graduates and undergraduates; special educational and subsistence grants for veterans, scholarships for their orphans; fellowships for graduate and postdoctoral work in science, mathematics, foreign languages, health sciences, and so forth; scholarships for Indians; loans for Cuban refugees, and so on. The programs are administered either by the agency involved or the college or university.

The agencies, departments, and bureaus involved in the conduct of such programs are numerous. The Veterans Administration, in 1959–60, in all programs aided 50,845 persons at a cost of $73,659,000—quite a contrast to 1947–48 when 1,235,761 students were in higher institutions under VA programs. Of this sum, almost 17 percent was spent for the rapidly expanding War Orphans Scholarship Program. The U.S. Office, in 1960–61, provided for 3,000 Defense and Language Fellowships about $7,447,000 and for 151,000 NDEA loans, about $73 million. NIH Fellowships in the same year numbered 4,205 at a cost of $19,-835,000. AEC awarded 353 fellowships at a cost of about $1 million, and NSF, through its various fellowship programs, aided about 4,197 persons at a cost of roughly $13 million. Scholarships for 632 Indians cost the Government $250,000 in 1960–61. Fellowships for the study of the mentally retarded aided, in 1959–60, about 175 individuals at a

[23] J. Kenneth Little, "Higher Education and National Purpose," *Educational Record*, XLII (July 1961), 161–72.

cost of $1 million. The Office of Vocational Rehabilitation fellowships aided 1,586 at a cost of $3,010,000.[24]

These programs in toto assisted about 212,468 undergraduates at a cost of $146,909,000 and 13,516 graduates at a cost of about $45 million. One needs no slide rule to see that, though the sums are much larger on the undergraduate side, the aid per individual assisted averaged $690 per undergraduate and over $3,000 per individual graduate student.[25] It should also be noted that nearly half the sum for undergraduates was for loans, whereas virtually all the funds for graduate students were in the form of grants, fellowships, or other types of funds for which no return was required. Missing from this analysis are the new NASA awards, which could in time add considerable to this total.

## Conclusion

In summary, then, the situation looks much like this: The area of research contributes to the support of students probably as much as $80 million; the area of education and training, $73 million; international activities, $22.54 million; and student financial assistance, $191 million—a grand total of $366.54 million.

For a slightly different perspective, let us look at the data categorized by the major departments and agencies to see whence the greatest support for the various types of personal educational subventions is coming. The amounts and order of magnitude are: [26]

| | |
|---|---|
| U.S. Office of Education . . . . | $ 87,320,000 |
| Veterans Administration . . . . | 73,000,000 |
| Public Health Service (National Institutes of Health) . . . . . | 69,800,000 |
| Department of Defense . . . . | 55,850,000 |
| Department of State . . . . . | 22,540,000 |
| National Science Foundation . . . | 45,760,000 |
| Total . . . . . . . . | $354,270,000 |

The balance up to $366,540,000 is accounted for by various other small programs and unallocated research funds from agencies such as NASA and the Department of Agriculture.

[24] Moon, *op. cit.*
[25] All veterans and NDEA loan recipients were classified as undergraduates.
[26] Research assistantships have been apportioned according to the percentages reported in Little, *A Survey of Federal Programs in Higher Education—Summary.*

Another analysis, according to aid form, produces some interesting patterns. In order these are:

| | |
|---|---:|
| Subsistence grants | $144,645,000 |
| Research assistantships | 80,000,000 |
| Loans | 73,000,000 |
| Fellowships | 46,355,000 |
| Foreign students | 22,540,000 |
| Total | $366,540,000 |

It was not easy to compile the data herein reported. Even more difficult, however, is the task of trying to reduce it to a set of meaningful generalizations with the hope of achieving succinct description of the present and glimpses, even if myopic, of what the future may hold in store. With the realization that for every generalization presented there may be as many examples to disprove as to prove it, I shall proceed.

1. Generally speaking Federal student aid efforts have been aimed at solving specific, immediate, and readily visible governmental or well-documented national manpower needs. But one should not conclude from this that there is any comprehensive policy governing Government student aid efforts—there is none.

2. Over half of the Federal funds going to the support of students are administered by institutions of higher learning. The expense of this administration to the institutions for certain types of programs may grow to be intolerable, particularly where loan collections and cancellations are involved. Virtually no use has been made of states for this purpose.

3. The concentration of Federal funds in the sciences has created not only imbalances between science and the humanities but imbalances within the sciences as well. For example, these funds have aided in drawing the best graduate students into research and away from teaching services and thereby have contributed to a decline in the quality of undergraduate science instruction particularly at the major universities.

4. There is considerable evidence to suggest that many agencies are, in view of the general nature of the programs they support, in competition with each other for the services of the same students in the same institutions. The need for greater coordination and cooperation at the Federal level between many of the agencies is obvious.

5. In a period of about fifteen years, Federal student support for undergraduates has shifted from the provision of almost complete support for over 50 percent of the student population (GI bill) to loaning money to no more than 5 percent of the student population (NDEA loan program) for on the average less than 30 percent of their costs.

6. Also in the same period of fifteen years the breadth of Federal support for students has shifted from a neutral position, according to the type of institutional or study program supported, to a position heavily favoring science and the support of public institutions.

7. The breadth and diversity of Federal student support programs across units of Government suggest how difficult must be their coordination within institutions which must either administer the programs and/or deal with agencies of Government in their conduct.

8. Though the total aid available to undergraduates through the colleges has been enhanced considerably by the NDEA loan program, these funds have failed to bring the nation's total aid available per undergraduate (when combined with college funds) up to the point where it was in 1955–56.[27]

9. The various forms in which Federal aid is provided to students suggest a philosophy implicit if not explicit that graduate education should be free to the individual but that undergraduate education should be supported extensively by those who receive it.

10. Federal aid for undergraduates thus far has failed to instill any real national concern for the value and necessity for excellence in pre-college preparation, whereas most programs at the graduate level are distinct promoters of excellence in undergraduate studies.

11. One must conclude from the evidence at hand that Federal programs of student assistance are significant instruments of institutional, as well as individual, support. The reasons for this conclusion are these: the majority of funds are administered (controlled) by institutions; they grow out of specialized educational or other services of a particular institution, and in many instances make them possible in the first place; many programs provide subsidy or overrides to institutions which admit these federally aided students.

The breadth and depth of Federal student support is indeed amazing.

[27] Rexford G. Moon, Jr., "Demand on Aid Funds Means More Planning," *Financial Aid News*, Vol. II, May 1962.

Considering the extent of this present commitment, there seems to be adequate evidence that Federal student aid is something to be welcomed and expected. Also considering the Federal commitment to student support efforts, it is not unreasonable to expect that some of the needed, increased Federal support of higher education in the future should come in one or more forms of student aid. After all, the support of individuals, as opposed to the direct support of institutions, is potentially much freer from church-state problems. Also the possibility of Federal influence on the educational process is minimized in the subvention of individuals in contrast to the direct support of institutions or of institutionally performed services. Support of individuals maximizes the individual's freedom of choice of program of study or institution, which is consistent with our political and educational aims. The problems of concentration of funds in institutions can be more equitably controlled through the support of students than through the purchase of services in institutions.

This method also makes it possible to put more emphasis on the need for, and desirability of quality preparation in, precollege work. Too, manpower concerns and needs and socioeconomic inequities can be more rapidly met and corrected through student support activities than through only institutional support. Continuing general programs of student support may be expected to cut down the attrition of students from our colleges, an area where there is a severe but unrecognized loss of talent. Last, and by no means least, from the strictly political point of view we might well expect our colleagues in the secondary and elementary schools to support the development of more such programs, for if families can be assured of partial assistance with college costs, they may be more willing to support the necessary improvements in plant and salaries at the local level than they are now.

Whether aid to students is really also aid to institutions is not the point for debate. I do believe, however, that a strong case can be made to show that it is. Aid to students, however, is aid to education. As educators, we must remember that institutions, as important as they are, are supportive to the educational process—they are not educational ends in themselves. At times we must appear very mercenary while seemingly putting the needs of institutions narrowly defined ahead of the needs of education broadly defined. I trust we do this occasionally because of our inability to awaken appropriate national concern for our institutional problems by more appropriate but possibly too esoteric means. Education concerns students and institutions, and the support of both must be our constant concern. What supports students, supports education; what supports education is beneficial to our institutions.

The evidence is clear that, at least in student aid matters, relationships between higher institutions and Government have been good. The principle has been established implicitly, if not explicitly, that the Federal Government has a responsibility to respond to national problems and worries through student aid means if such methods will assist. It disturbs me, therefore, to discover that even though educators and politicians have in the past found, in the words of Jefferson, accord for their differences, in the matter of scholarships for undergraduates such accord still seems as far in the future as Jefferson's words are in our past.

# FEDERAL PROGRAMS OF LOANS AND GRANTS FOR CAPITAL IMPROVEMENTS

*Clarence Scheps*
VICE-PRESIDENT AND COMPTROLLER,
TULANE UNIVERSITY

E XPANDING ENROLLMENTS, EVER-INCREASING DEMANDS BY GOVERNMENT and industry for services in defense-related areas, increasing pressures for expansion of graduate instruction, growing emphasis on medical research, and with a painful awareness of the inadequacy of present physical facilities—all these enable one to understand higher education's great concern and interest in capital improvements—land, buildings, and equipment.

The task at this session is to present information on Federal participation in capital improvements. In doing so, we shall briefly review past and present programs of the Federal Government in this area, describe current proposals for capital improvements now before the Congress, and attempt to elicit discussion on such questions as: Is Federal assistance needed in the provision of capital facilities? If assistance is needed and desirable, what are the principal obstacles in the path of obtaining such assistance?

## Federal Programs of Aid for Capital Improvements

Federal programs of loans and grants to colleges and universities for capital improvements are a relatively new development which has grown to considerable proportions in recent years and continues to grow in significance. The first Federal activity of any consequence involving capital improvements in educational institutions was the depression-born WPA and PWA programs. Assistance to education was incidental to the primary purpose of these programs, which was to provide employment to victims of the depression. This matching program was limited to public institutions and, in all, provided $111 million for 664 building projects on college campuses.

Another program, generated in part by a Federal problem, was that sponsored by the Federal Public Housing Administration after World War II and designed to assist institutions of higher learning in accommodating the veterans returning to the campuses in large numbers under the GI Bill of Rights. This extremely valuable program provided the institutions with temporary housing for single and married students —some of it still in use. Another part of the same program involved the conversion of war surplus buildings into temporary classrooms and offices.

It is emphasized that in both of these early programs, Federal participation was prompted by considerations other than general aid to education.

Current Federal programs involving loans and grants to educational institutions for capital improvements may be classified and discussed under several headings—namely, the Surplus Property Program, the Urban Renewal Program, miscellaneous programs, the College Housing Loan Program and research programs.

### SURPLUS PROPERTY PROGRAM

The Surplus Property Program was authorized first in 1919 after World War I and was continued and expanded following World War II. Under this program, property no longer needed by the Government can be sold or transferred to educational institutions at a fraction of original cost. It is estimated that since 1947, $250 million of real and personal property has been transferred to the colleges and universities under this program.

### URBAN RENEWAL PROGRAM

Of considerable value to higher education have been changes in the Urban Renewal Act, which, under certain circumstances, provide a method by which colleges and universities may obtain land adjacent to campuses. Since the Federal Government participates in the acquisition cost, institutions are able to acquire land through their local urban renewal organizations at much lower cost than otherwise would be possible. Moreover, the program enables the institution to obtain land which otherwise could be acquired only through the exercise of eminent domain, a right not available to all institutions.

A third type of current assistance includes a number of programs, the purposes of which are not to aid educational institutions but to serve a special purpose of a particular governmental agency. An example is the Area Development Program under which the Federal Government has, in a few instances, financed the construction of buildings for institutions of higher learning, where such construction has contributed to the major purpose of the Area Development Act— to assist depressed areas.

The two chief programs of interest to colleges and universities in the area of capital improvements are the College Housing Loan Program and a large variety of research programs sponsored by many agencies of the Government.

Since more than 70 percent of the eligible colleges and universities in the nation already are participating in the College Housing Loan Program, inaugurated in 1950, it needs little discussion in this group. It is specifically designed to assist colleges and universities in the housing of students and faculty, and to provide facilities related to such housing, including food service, infirmaries, and student unions. The Federal Government assists the institutions by providing loans, for periods up to fifty years, at low rates of interest. The interest rate is set by a formula written into the law and varies with the prevailing rate at which the Treasury is able to borrow money for its own purposes. This rate has fluctuated from a low of 2¾ percent to a current high, as of July 1, 1962, of 3½ percent. To date, this program has made available 1,925 loans totaling about $2 billion. These loans have enabled the colleges and universities to provide housing accommodations for more than 400,000 students, faculty, nurses, and interns. In addition, they have assisted in the financing of some 500 student unions, dining facilities, and infirmaries.

The program, somewhat uniquely, has had the unqualified and at times militant support of all of higher education and, except for a short period of time during the Eisenhower administration, it has had the support of the executive and legislative branches of the Government. In the opinion of many observers, the College Housing Loan Program, supervised by the Housing and Home Finance Agency, is one of the most competently managed and effective programs of assistance to higher education ever sponsored by the Federal Government. The 1961 Congress extended the program for four years, with funds provided at an annual rate of $300 million.

RESEARCH PROGRAMS

It is believed that nearly every department of the Federal Government is authorized to finance research on college campuses. Frequently, such research support may include assistance in the acquisition of capital improvements. A partial list of governmental agencies that seem to be authorized to finance research would include Department of Agriculture, Federal Aviation Agency, Department of Commerce, National Bureau of Standards, Office of Civil and Defense Mobilization, Department of the Interior, Post Office Department, Small Business Administration, Department of State, and Veterans Administration. Most of these agencies are concerned with research only incidentally, as far as the colleges and universities are concerned. Those agencies which have programs of substantial import to education include the National Science Foundation, Department of Defense, Department of Health, Education, and Welfare, Atomic Energy Commission, and National Aeronautics and Space Administration. Following is a brief description of programs of these agencies involving capital improvements:

1. The *National Science Foundation,* which does business almost entirely with educational institutions, provides grants for the construction of highly specialized research facilities, for the renovation of laboratories used for graduate instruction, and for the acquisition of laboratory equipment. The most important program of the Foundation, involving physical facilities, began in 1960 and provides matching grants for construction, renovation, and equipping of graduate-level research laboratories in engineering and in the natural sciences. In 1961, grants for these purposes of over $2 million were made to fifty-four institutions. There is every indication that the participation of the National Science Foundation in financing capital improvements on college campuses will increase substantially in the years ahead.

The National Science Foundation participates also in the financing of expensive and specialized equipment for the joint use of groups of universities—for example, the radio telescope at Greenbank, West Virginia.

2. The *Department of Defense,* through its various offices in the Army, Navy, and Air Force, has devoted increasingly large sums of money to research programs, many of which provide funds for capital improvements. These programs range from small project grants, in which funds may be available for construction, alteration, and equipment, to the independent research center, which is financed in full by the Federal Government but is operated by an educational institution. An example of the latter is the Jet Propulsion Laboratory operated for the National Aeronautics and Space Administration by the California Institute of Technology.

3. The *Department of Health, Education, and Welfare* has a number of programs involving grants for capital improvements to colleges and universities. By far the major portion of these programs relate to research in medicine and are administered by the National Institutes of Health, which is part of the U.S. Public Health Service. Under the direction of this department is the Health Research Facilities Act of 1956, which provides $30 million a year to colleges and universities on a fifty-fifty matching basis for the construction and equipping of research facilities in schools of medicine, dentistry, public health, nursing, and such health-related fields as biology, zoology, and psychology. To date, $209 million has been awarded to educational institutions under this program.

In many other programs sponsored by the National Institutes of Health, funds are available for construction, renovation, and equipment. These programs range from relatively small grants for research on a project basis to the increasingly large center programs in which NIH may finance the acquisition of land, the construction of buildings, and the purchase of equipment necessary to the operation of these centers. Intermediate programs include the various clinical center research programs, in which funds are available on a nonmatching basis for the remodeling and refurbishing of existing medical and hospital buildings and for highly specialized and expensive equipment. In 1961–62 it is estimated that NIH expended in excess of $100 million for capital improvements in institutions of higher learning.

Other divisions of the Department of Health, Education, and Welfare, especially the Office of Education, have programs involving capital improvements, limited for the most part to equipment.

4. The *Atomic Energy Commission,* under the authority of the Atomic Energy Commission Act of 1954, is empowered to make grants to educational institutions for the acquisition of equipment to be used in courses of study in the general area of nuclear fission and technology. The general purpose of these grants is to assist the institutions in producing scientists trained in radiation biology and in the use of isotopes. Unlike most other government programs, this program has as its announced purpose the improvement of teaching, not the production of research. AEC is involved in other programs ranging from project grants to the large research center financed by the Government and managed by a university.

5. The *National Aeronautics and Space Administration* has broad authority from the Congress which, it is believed, will include provision of funds to colleges and universities for substantial programs of capital improvements. Since the agency is relatively in its infancy, the details of its programs in these areas are not yet known. It is likely, however, to become extremely important in assisting colleges and universities in expanding facilities in science and engineering.

In analyzing the intent and objectives of the currently existing Federal programs for capital improvements, it is noted that except for the College Housing Loan Program, all of these programs originated for or were prompted by some prevailing Federal interest—usually in national defense or in national health. Moreover, most of the programs are related to research and not to instruction. Even the College Housing Loan Program at its outset had overtones of national defense in that the need for housing had to be justified in these terms. After the end of the Korean War, this provision was dropped.

It is emphasized that no current program of the Federal Government is directly concerned with loans and grants to educational institutions for library and classroom purposes, nor is the avowed purpose of any current Federal program general assistance to higher education.

## Proposals Before the 1962 Congress

The 1962 Congress had two major proposals before it involving general assistance to colleges and universities for capital improvements.

The first was the so-called academic facilities bill, represented by HR 8900 and S 1241, and the health professions educational assistance bill, HR 4999.

With respect to the academic facilities bill, it is interesting to note that although both Houses of Congress, by overwhelming majorities, approved bills providing construction aid to education, no final action has yet been effected. The House version of the academic facilities bill included loans and grants to all eligible colleges and passed the House on January 30, 1962. The Senate version, which was passed on February 6, 1962, included grants only to two-year community colleges and loans for four-year colleges and universities. It also included provision for Federal scholarships. The House bill was prevented from going to conference for several months by the Rules Committee but was cleared for conference on May 9. The conferees met for the first time on June 19, finally reported the bill on September 19. On September 20, the House voted to recommit the bill to conference. The action to recommit, in effect, killed the bill for the session. Both bills were on a matching basis and each provided a total of $300 million a year in assistance for academic facilities.

The health professions educational assistance bill, HR 4999, provided $75 million a year in matching grants for the construction of teaching facilities in medical, dental, osteopathic, and public health schools. It also included a provision of $50 million a year on a matching basis for health research facilities. The bill was approved by the House Committee on Interstate and Foreign Commerce, was cleared by the Rules Committee, but failed to receive consideration of the full House.

## The Needs for the Future

Let us now briefly explore the questions suggested at the outset of this paper. Is Federal assistance needed for the expansion of facilities in our colleges and universities? What have been the obstacles that up to now have prevented general assistance for capital improvements?

Each of the several studies that have been made in recent years has rendered the firm conclusion that participation by the Federal Government is essential if the necessary capital facilities are to be provided for higher education in the years immediately ahead. The President's Committee on Education Beyond the High School found that Federal assistance would be needed and strongly recommended that a program be initiated. A comprehensive study by the U.S. Office of Education indicated that, between 1960 and 1970, $19 billion would be needed by the colleges and universities for capital improvements and that other sources of financing available to higher education would not be sufficient to provide the capital facilities needed. A study by the American Council on Education reached the same conclusion and, in part, led the Council to propose to the Congress and to vigorously support a loan and grant program for capital improvements.

A survey just published by the Office of Education reports that colleges and universities are planning $7.5 billion for new construction, renovation, and campus improvements to be completed by the fall of 1965. With regard to the all-important question of how this capital outlay program is to be financed, the institutions were unable to identify the source of about 20 percent of the funds necessary to complete the building programs. It is reasonable to expect that this unknown source of financing was expected to be the Federal Government.

Faced with ever-mounting operational needs other than capital outlay, and recognizing that there will be increases in other sources available to education, such as student fees, voluntary contributions, and state and local appropriations—there is no doubt in this speaker's mind that if we are to accomplish the job, the gap will have to be filled through Federal action.

The case for greatly increased Federal participation in capital improvements has been made thoroughly. What, then, accounts for the failures to bring about congressional implementation of this program? It appears that a number of obstacles have prevented the enactment of legislation in the 1962 Congress. Among these can be listed the following:

1. The issue of church and state. Although there have been opinions advanced by many, including the President of the United States, that assistance for physical facilities to church-related institutions is not unconstitutional, this issue continues to be an important obstacle to the passage of aid to higher education. Many Congressmen, who basically oppose further expansion of Federal interest in education, have seized upon the church-state issue to oppose current measures designed to assist higher education. There is no doubt that this is one of the reasons why major legislation was not enacted in 1962.

2. The private versus public issue: Despite efforts of the American Council on Education to present a united front, some educational organizations strongly opposed Federal grants to private institutions of higher learning. Opposition has been expressed by the N.E.A., and by several organizations not directly affiliated with higher education, such as the Council of Chief State School Officers. Historically, no Federal program for aid to higher education authorized by the Congress has ever made any distinction between public and private institutions of higher education. The American Council on Education in its booklet entitled *The Need to Close Ranks in Higher Education* emphasized the necessity of presenting a united front. The Council stated: "the crucial issue is not how many dollars come from private sources and how many from public sources but whether or not the total of these dollars will be sufficient to meet the challenge colleges and universities face. The basic choice for the people of our country is between expenditures for higher education and expenditures for other needs." If history is any guide, there will be no Federal aid to higher education unless such assistance can be made to all types of institutions without respect to affiliation or control.

3. Opposition to Federal support to higher education: Perhaps the most fundamental reason why there has been no major Federal aid to higher education is the basic and instinctive objection felt deeply by many, including those in education, to the general proposition of Federal support to higher education. There are a great many sincere individuals who are concerned over any possibility of Federal control over our schools and colleges. Educators themselves have not fully made up their minds in many cases. Trustees, although frequently pleased when their presidents manage to obtain assistance from Washington, publicly express opposition to Federal support of higher education. There still has not been a wholehearted acceptance of the fact that the Federal Government is already deeply involved in financing higher education and probably will be much more so in the years ahead. Significantly, however, it is in the area of assistance for capital improvements that there is the least general opposition and it is in this area that the greatest chance of success prevails.

This speaker shares the concern which some feel about Federal aid to education. There is overwhelming evidence, however, that the needs of higher education are so great, that the need for improving the quality of higher education is so essential to the welfare of this nation, that these factors transcend all other considerations. If, in fact, higher education does close ranks, there is every reason to believe that a sensible program of assistance in the area of capital improvements can be forthcoming.

# THE FEDERAL RESEARCH ENDEAVOR
# AND HIGHER EDUCATION

*John C. Weaver*

VICE-PRESIDENT FOR RESEARCH AND DEAN
OF THE GRADUATE COLLEGE,
STATE UNIVERSITY OF IOWA

THE TOPIC, OR SPRAWLING CLUSTER OF INTERWOVEN TOPICS, WHICH this specific session is asked to bring into some measure of focus, is the vast and uncoordinated array of relationships between the Federal research endeavor and higher education. Since a good three-quarters of all the income presently received by our colleges and universities from the several agencies in Washington is assigned to the support of research activities, it is readily apparent that we, in this particular gathering, have been allotted a more than ample share of the total concern of the Council's 1962 Annual Meeting.

Whether or not I could possibly *know* enough to cover my subject completely, I am confronted with another limiting circumstance which further complicates my problem and which I should make clear to you. An inadequate fund of solid, factual knowledge can sometimes be effectively disguised by slipping quickly into high verbal gear to raise issues, to view with alarm, and to make sonorous pronouncements based merely, if ever so elusively, on personal opinions born of the prejudice of the completely ignorant. But consider, if you will, that Dr. Babbidge, when outlining my assignment back in July, wrote: "The important thing to keep in mind is that we have given you an essentially descriptive job. . . . All discussion of the impact of these [Federal] programs on institutions and all discussion of other issues that flow from Federal involvement, are to be deferred. . . . Thus, you are . . . positively discouraged from dealing with issues." How could one make it more difficult for a speaker than to permit him to discuss facts without expressing opinions? Perhaps there is one narrow loophole which Dr. Babbidge, inadvertently, hasn't drawn completely shut.

Sometimes by the adroit arrangements of facts, one can effectively imply opinions or create issues without really being caught at his nefarious game.

I must apologize in advance for what will seem a plethora of figures and a recitation of factual material, but these are inherent in the nature of my topic. My attempt will be to establish a framework for the discussions that follow. But before taking the measure of our present position, we might, in the interests of perspective, look back for a moment. As someone has shrewdly suggested, the primary trouble with each generation is that it hasn't read the minutes of the last meeting!

Many among the concerned spectators of the contemporary scene seem to presume that an interest on the part of our national Government in research and the quest for new and useful knowledge is a mid-twentieth century phenomenon that has, as a result of some caprice, appeared full-blown among us without background or warning. Just a moment of sober reflection, however, should dispel any such misconception. A Republic with fathers like Franklin and Jefferson needed no century and a half to sense its stake in science and discovery. Jefferson was as ready to use Federal subsidy to launch Lewis and Clark into the unknown in 1804 as the National Aeronautics and Space Administration has been to provide similar aid to Glenn and Schirra in 1962, and the basic reasons in 1804 were essentially the same as those in 1962.

Think back a moment over a selection of some of the significant evidences of our Federal Government's continuing concern, both for life on the frontiers of knowledge and for the general welfare of education. For example, in 1846, Congress created the Smithsonian Institution to further scientific research, exhibition, and publication. Even under the overpowering preoccupations of Civil War, the enduring and imaginative influence of the Morrill Act was brought into being in 1862, and the National Academy of Sciences was born in 1863. There followed the establishment of the United States Office of Education in 1867, and the passage of the Hatch Act, with its initiation of a highly effective institutional grant system through our Agricultural Experiment Stations in 1887. The Second Morrill Act came in 1890.

The present National Aeronautics and Space Administration was foreshadowed in the founding of the National Advisory Committee for Aeronautics in 1915. This same year witnessed the formation of the Naval Consulting Board, and 1916 brought the organization of the National Research Council within the National Academy of Sciences. The Smith-Hughes Act in support of vocational education was passed in 1917.

In the fast-moving years that followed, two world wars further reinforced the nation's understanding of its dependence upon the scientific and technological resources of its people. The unassailable reality of need and aspiration, of survival itself, at the end of World War II culminated in the creation of such powerful manifestations of research determination as the Atomic Energy Commission and the Office of Naval Research in 1946 and the National Science Foundation in 1950.

The growth of the Federal subsidy for research and development in the last two decades has occurred at a constantly accelerating rate, and in recent days has achieved awesome proportions. So also has the massive interdependence of the Federal Government and our institutions of higher education. Joined, as they increasingly have been, by considerations of capability and need in research, their interdependence has, with almost meteoric swiftness, been driven to new levels of magnitude. Nonetheless, dramatic, bold, and significant as these more recent developments have been, it is well to remember that they are not without clearly discernible evolutionary roots in a considerable soil of established precedent.

## Sources and Amounts of Federal Research Spending

Caught up as we are in an age of science and technology, where "atoms," "orbits," "research," and "discovery" are magic words, when we are losing ourselves in both the infinitesimally small and the infinitely vast, we are expending our financial substance in figures almost as unintelligible as the unknowns we are exploring. In the decade 1951 to 1961, the governments, industries, colleges, universities, and a variety of nonacademic, nonprofit institutions in this country spent an aggregate of $80 billion for research and development activities. This staggering total outlay, inclusive of an expenditure for the year 1961–62 of $15 billion, is almost exactly comparable to our total national budget in the fiscal year 1961. In the first year of this $80 billion decade, our Federal Government contributed about half the total of the nation's research and development funds. By the end of the ten-year period, the share paid by Washington had assumed its present magnitude of two-thirds.

In the late 1930's, the Federal Government was budgeting annually on the order of $100 million for all of its programs in research and development. By 1950, this had risen to $1.1 billion. In 1960, it was $8.1 billion; in 1961, $9.2 billion. For fiscal 1963, the present estimate for the Federal obligations for research and development is *$12.4* billion. These are sobering figures, but of one thing we can be certain: we are only in the foothills today; the peaks of these mountains are still hidden in the clouds far above us.

To narrow these Federal expenditures for research and development to the areas directly significant to our educational enterprise calls for several steps in refinement. First, let us note that of the total number of Federal dollars devoted to the general category of research and development, about one-quarter goes to the support of research (both basic and applied) and about three-quarters to development activities. Some twenty-five major arms of the Government are identified by the National Science Foundation as being involved in budgetary obligations for research and development work, but a bit more than 90 percent of the total is accounted for within just four agencies: Department of Defense; Department of Health, Education, and Welfare; Atomic Energy Commission; and National Aeronautics and Space Administration. The next four agencies, in the order of expenditure, are: Department of Agriculture, Department of the Interior, Federal Aviation Agency, and National Science Foundation. Even though listing these as the second four, we should bear in mind that together they represent less than 5 percent of the total Federal financial obligation in the field of research and development.

Further, it should be observed that the total research and development program of the Federal Government can be divided between that portion which is undertaken intramurally in Federal installations by Federal employees, and that portion carried on extramurally for the Government by such organizations as industrial firms and educational institutions. Taking the total of $9.2 billion for research and development in fiscal 1961 as an example, 22 percent of the funds were spent in intramural operations as against 78 percent in extramural activities. Of the 78 percentage points devoted in 1961 to extramural work, 63 are identified with profit-making organizations, such as industrial firms and commercial laboratories, 11 with educational institutions, and the remaining four with other types of organizations.

## Federal Spending for Research in Higher Institutions

Thus, we can state that currently 11 percent of the over-all Federal spending for research and development directly concerns our educational establishment. In actual dollars this meant $964 million in fiscal 1961, and it is estimated that the total will be approximately $1.2 billion in fiscal 1962. These figures include, it should be noted, the very sizable funds which support Federal contract research centers under the administrative supervision of universities, such as the Argonne National Laboratory of the University of Chicago, the Los Alamos Scientific Laboratory supervised by the University of California, and the Applied Physics Laboratory of the Johns Hopkins University. In 1961, $401 million, or just over 40 percent of the total expended by the Federal Government for research and development in our educational institutions, was devoted to the maintenance of such Federal contract research centers. If these centers are eliminated from consideration, the Federal outlay in direct support of research and development (and we can hope there is not too much of the latter!) in our colleges and universities amounted to $563 million in 1961; $732 million in 1962.

Of the total of an estimated $1.2 billion spent extramurally by the Federal Government in our educational institutions in 1962, better than 95 percent came from five primary agencies. Twenty-seven percent of the total came from the Atomic Energy Commission; 24 percent from the Department of Defense; 23 percent from the Department of Health, Education, and Welfare; 13 percent from the National Aeronautics and Space Administration; and 8 percent from the National Science Foundation.

At this juncture we should narrow our field of observation still further. Let us now eliminate from consideration those funds that are devoted to development work and clearly applied research, and center our attention on the segment of the pie that is of most legitimate and proper concern to the educational community, namely, the Federal funds spent in support of basic research. According to the National Science Foundation, the total Federal expenditure for basic research in fiscal 1961 was $969 million. Of this, 25 percent was spent intra-murally and 75 percent extramurally. Forty-one percent of the total, substantially better than half of the extramural portion, was committed to colleges and universities. Appropriately enough then, where basic research is concerned, our educational institutions for the first time have assumed the dominant role.

Interestingly enough, and—if Dr. Babbidge isn't listening, I'll sneak in a two-word opinion—*fortunately enough,* Federal expenditures for basic research appear to be growing at a rate faster than expenditures for applied research. An estimated 90 percent increase in Federal basic research support from $740 million in 1960 to over $1.4 billion in 1962, is significantly associated with the accelerating activities of the National Aeronautics and Space Administration. The impressive and rapidly expanding sums being committed to space flight programs, having no other objective than the increase of knowledge, involve enormous expenditures for launch vehicles that must be counted into the cost totals for basic research.

According to the National Science Foundation, thirteen major Federal agencies are engaged in the support of basic research. Five of them, in surprisingly comparable amounts, account for 97 percent of the commitments of this type to educational institutions. In fiscal 1961, $88 million, or 22 percent of the total, came from the Department of Health, Education, and Welfare; $85 million, or 21 percent, from the Atomic Energy Commission; $80 million, or 20 percent, from the Department of Defense; $72 million, or 18 percent, from the National Aeronautics and Space Administration; and $63 million, or 16 percent, from the National Science Foundation. Less than 3 percent of the total Federal support for basic research in our educational community, as defined by the National Science Foundation, was furnished by the next four most important contributors: Department of Agriculture; Department of Commerce; Department of the Interior; and Veterans Administration. In evaluating the relationships between these principal Federal subsidizers of basic research and our academic household, it is significant that only NASA and AEC show larger obligations to university-administered, Federal contract research centers than to the educational institutions proper.

Another footnote of more than passing interest in the educational scene is the fact that, whereas the relationship between the land-grant colleges and universities and the Department of Agriculture was the first really significant union of Federal and academic concerns in research, and really the only important one as recently as the beginning of World War II, the USDA is now in a relatively minor position among the Government agencies seeking research arrangements with our institutions of higher learning. Even among the land-grant schools themselves, no more than one-fourth to one-third of the Federal research dollars currently comes from the Department of Agriculture.

## Patterns of Distribution of Federal Research Funds

The potential for elaboration among these basic dimensions of the Federal involvement in the research affairs of our colleges and universities is almost limitless. Perhaps by way of untangling myself from all these complexities, it would be well for me to proceed to a quick and rather simple enumeration of a few additional facts. Hopefully, this will be an exercise in provocative suggestion rather than in tedious proliferation.

In reflection of the preoccupying pressures of our time, and of the fact that by and large the Federal extramural research program is really one of purchasing services rather than philanthropically aiding educational institutions, there is an enormous concentration of the research subsidy in the natural sciences. Of the 969 million Federal dollars spent in behalf of basic research in 1961, 71 percent was expended on projects in the physical sciences (including mathematics and engineering), 26 percent on projects in the life sciences (biological, medical, and agricultural), 2 percent on the psychological sciences, and 1 percent on the social sciences. The humanities are, with a few localized exceptions, forgotten! Among the life sciences the favored field is, of course, medicine—with its powerful backing from the United States Public Health Service. Among the physical sciences, the strong leader is engineering, concentrating its support in the form of powerful contracts and grants from the Department of Defense, the Atomic

Energy Commission, and the National Aeronautics and Space Administration.

Within the educational establishment, the colleges of engineering, medicine, and agriculture attract the greatest attention and support, a fact which reveals not only the overriding national concern for scientific advance, but the practically oriented emphasis of Government agencies with immediate and specific missions to accomplish. To be sure, there is a considerable range of difference among the Federal agencies in the manner in which they view their goals and define their areas of support. Basic research, for example, receives 100 percent of the funds of the National Science Foundation, but no more than 21 percent of the total financial resources for research and development within the Department of Defense.

The second among my concluding observations also has to do with a significant axis of concentration in the Federal research and development funds. It has already been observed that the Federal subsidies are dispensed by a relatively small number of primary agencies. We have further noted that there are striking imbalances among the fields of knowledge which are supported. To these considerations should now be added the fact that only a comparatively small number of our institutions of higher learning participate in a significant way in these extramural efforts of the Federal Government.

The kernel of the story is essentially as follows: There are somewhat more than two thousand colleges and universities in the United States. Among these, fewer than five hundred receive any federally sponsored research money whatever. More than two-thirds of all the Federal research funds channeled into our collegiate enterprise as a whole are received by twenty-five institutions. Fifty schools account for more than four-fifths of the total available funds, and one hundred institutions bring the percentage to about 95.

Viewing the matter geographically, a high level of regional concentration should be noted. It is an accurate generalization to say that most of the academically oriented Federal money in support of research is centered in: (a) a group of strong, private institutions in southern New England and the Mid-Atlantic seaboard; (b) a cluster of large state universities in the Middle West; and (c) a handful of highly developed private and public institutions on the Pacific Coast. The reasons for these patterns of institutional concentration are not hard to find. A research-minded Federal Government, seeking in the first instance to *use* rather than to *aid* higher education, logically patronizes those institutions in which it can command the highest quality and most effective services. This means that the Federal agencies turn most often to those universities which, over the years, have had the perception and the financial resources to build and hold faculties with great and unique talents. There are grave shortages of such high excellence, and the individual scholars who in the final analysis attract large Government subsidies are found heavily concentrated in a relatively small number of favored academic Shangri-Las.

Many observable and closely interrelated characteristics are found woven in intimate correlation around the principal academic citadels of Government research support. For example, these institutions are the primary centers of doctoral level graduate education, where uncommonly creative, research-minded faculties are not only engaged in the pursuit of their own probing along the frontiers of the unknown, but where graduate students—the researchers of tomorrow—congregate in unusual numbers as co-workers and apprentices. These are also the institutions that have had the foresight to support such professional interests as they may have had in medicine, engineering or agriculture, with powerful arrays of basic science departments, where the emphasis has been on fundamental research and nonprofessionally oriented education. These, too, are the institutions that reveal the presence of uniquely superior faculties by the numbers of postdoctoral fellows who cluster about their academic fires, and also by their dominating contributions to the various consultative and advisory bodies that the Government agencies utilize to aid them in the direction of their research and development missions.

There is one associated point here which is, I believe, both a fact which I am entitled to include, and an issue, which by definition, therefore, should not be the subject of expanded observation at this stage of the proceedings. The already strong and powerful institutions attract the lion's share of Federal research funds and, in so doing, become still stronger and more powerful. The weaker majority grow relatively still weaker. It is hard to see the end of this road, but the ever-expanding, virtually unassailable, bastions of intellectual power on a few towering heights are the most salient features of the current academic landscape. This fact must give pause to the thoughtful observer.

## Observations on the Distribution
## of Federal Research Funds

A third matter that deserves listing, if not extensive discussion, is the uncoordinated nature of the Government-university research relationship at both the granting and receiving ends of the financial pipeline. Some fifty arms of the Federal Government are dispensing funds of various types to institutions of collegiate level, and at least half of them are administering research funds. Nowhere in the Federal system is there any mechanism to monitor, create guiding policies, or, in any manner, coordinate these diverse activities, let alone any central group charged with the responsibility of occasionally brooding over the multifarious influences and impacts that are being created. The same lack of coordination of outlook and concern exists at the academic end of the line, where nearly five hundred independent institutions jostle one another uneasily at the trough they dare not see run dry. This fact is noted, for the question it asks is clear: Is not the importance of the relationship, the interdependent need, that exists between the Federal Government and our institutions of higher learning, now too vital to leave in an unattended and often almost bitterly competitive state of happenstance?

A fourth matter that needs to be cited for the record is the particular manner in which the research funds come from the Government agency to the college or university. The most common pattern has been the Federal purchase of a specific project proposal; a purchase made either under the terms of contract or a grant of dollars to cover a specified complex of work to be done in a given period of time. There is considerable evidence that, whereas the project system was workable in the earlier days of a limited Government-university relationship, the present range of activity has become so broad and massive that this cumbersome way of doing business should be sharply curtailed or abandoned altogether. In its place could be substituted, at least in part, the practice of institutional grants, with a return to the campus of many of the decisions that are now unfortunately made at detached distance in Washington. The National Science Foundation and the Public Health Service are two agencies that have already taken first steps in this direction.

Fifth, and finally, one could hardly conclude a summation of the present state of the Federal-university relationship in research without a word about the indirect costs of research—overhead. For many years the academic community has argued that if our institutions are to undertake federally sponsored research, the fully audited overhead costs should be paid by the sponsor. The several Government agencies have responded in a variety of ways, from allowing total negotiated costs to various formulas permitting fixed percentages of total direct costs.

Perhaps it can be argued that the research funds received from the Government are so helpful to our institutions that we should be willing to shoulder a certain measure of the indirect cost involved, but there can be no doubt that full reimbursement is not being made and that substantial involvement in Government research inevitably represents heavy drains on already inadequate institutional resources. For example, at my own institution, a modest participant in federally sponsored research, my records show that collectible overhead on the Federal grant requests made by the University of Iowa for the first six months of this year fall nearly one-half million dollars short of what would be produced by the rates accepted by the Federal auditor in our local situation. This is a more serious diversion of institutional funds than is either generally appreciated or easily defended.

These, then, are the general contours and essential characteristics of the current Federal programs in research as I see them. Surely among such facts and figures and among the many others of which you certainly are aware, there is no shortage of issues awaiting definition and discussion. The stakes are high; the wild cards are numerous; the players are both able and dedicated. I urge that we bring our most perceptive insight and creative attention to bear on the pressing problems of the game.

# FEDERAL PROGRAMS OF EDUCATION AND TRAINING

*J. Kenneth Little*

PROFESSOR OF EDUCATIONAL PSYCHOLOGY,
UNIVERSITY OF WISCONSIN

THE INTEREST OF THE FEDERAL GOVERNMENT IN PROGRAMS OF EDUCATION and training is wide, diverse, long-standing, and growing. Profound and fast-moving forces of scientific advance and international ferment are spelling a growing interdependence between Federal agencies and departments and institutions of higher education and a closer identification of the services of colleges and universities with the accomplishment of specific national objectives. The extraordinary contingencies of our age increasingly call for extraordinary minds which have had extraordinary educational training and experience. Tomorrow's world of work will require a more flexible and mobile labor force, educated and trained to higher levels of competence. The complexity and urgency of national and international problems dictate the necessity for cultivating higher levels of information, intelligence, and understanding among all citizens.

National interests and purposes now have international overtones. The values we hold about the dignity of man and the importance of education for free, self-governing peoples are valid for all humanity. The extension of these values to the peoples of new and developing nations is now a part of the national purpose and a new frontier of educational service.

Very briefly expressed, this is the backdrop against which federally sponsored activities in higher education are to be viewed. The sponsorship of educational and training programs by agencies and departments of the Federal Government is a natural outgrowth of specifically expressed national objectives. The participation of colleges and universities in the federally sponsored programs is a natural consequence of their purposes and resources as educational institutions.

Certain common purposes are apparent within most federally sponsored programs. These purposes are: (1) to take full advantage of the nation's present resources of specialized personnel, knowledge, and research capacity for the accomplishment of specific national objectives; (2) to strengthen and expand these resources as needed for the accomplishment of specific national objectives; and (3) to encourage and assist larger numbers of American youth to continue their education to levels which are consistent with their individual potential; especially to increase the number and improve the quality of the nation's supply of persons with high-level technical, scientific, engineering, and other professional training.

The accomplishment of such purposes is a part of the mission of most Federal departments and agencies. The educational interests and the activities of the Federal Government, as a whole, are practically as broad as the Government itself; but the missions of Federal departments and agencies usually have specific purposes in limited fields as defined by legislation or by executive directive. Most federally sponsored programs are not conceived as aids to institutions of higher education, in the usual connotation of the term "Federal aid." Instead, the programs are directed toward the accomplishment of certain objectives in science, engineering, technology, health, agriculture, world affairs, or other expressed national goals.

## Patterns of the Federal-Institutional Relationship

Over the years, two major patterns of relationship between the Federal Government and institutions of higher education have emerged.

The first is a pattern of Federal-state cooperation. In this pattern, the Federal Government joins with the states in support of educational programs directed toward the achievement of a specific goal deemed to be in the national interest. The Federal Government provides continuing appropriations for use in institutions established or designated by the states for the accomplishment of these goals. This plan is exemplified in the nation's land-grant colleges which this year are celebrating the 100th anniversary of their establishment. This relationship has proved effective for its purpose, and this set of colleges now constitutes a major resource for many missions of Federal departments and agencies.

The second pattern—that of Federal-institutional cooperation—evolved out of practices developed during war periods in which facilities and specialized personnel were needed for military or defense-related purposes, and a procedure of contracting for the needed educational and research services of colleges and universities was developed. This experience, coupled with that of administering the GI educational benefits, provided precedent for the extension of such arrangements to other types of Federal programs and purposes. These procedures have enabled privately sponsored as well as public institutions to participate, and have enabled Federal agencies and departments to locate their activities in any willing institution which has the facilities, resources, or location needed to produce the desired services with excellence, efficiency, and dispatch.

The National Defense Education Act of 1958 demonstrated a trend toward a more broadly defined Federal interest in higher education. The miscellany of programs established under its provisions retains the contract and grant procedures for programs in specified fields, but, in addition, seeks to broaden and strengthen the nation's resources in graduate education, to increase the supply of college teachers, and to stimulate college attendance by providing student loans.

It is important to observe that each Federal department and agency formulates its own policies and procedures and establishes its own relationships with institutions of higher education. Federal departments and agencies report to different committees of the Congress and operate under differing legislative and executive directives. Likewise, each of the many institutions of higher education makes its own policies and forms its own relationships with Federal departments and agencies. In fact, the global terms "higher education" and "Federal Government" have in this context no operational meaning. Each set of units operates plurally and without an over-all policy or mechanism which coordinates its relationships with the other. The absence of a single policy or coordinating mechanism results in part from the values placed upon diversity and individuality among institutions of higher education, and partly from a general resistance to centralized authority in education.

## Types of Federally Sponsored Programs
## of Education and Training

The specific purpose of this paper is to report in broad perspective and in general dimensions the trends and policies of federally sponsored programs of education and training. Certain definitions and limitations of the programs to be covered will be helpful. This discussion concentrates upon only those programs in which a Federal agency or department makes a formal arrangement with a college or university for the performance of a specialized educational service determined by the Federal agency or department. This classification of programs is, of course, somewhat arbitrary. It is helpful to consider that Federal programs of education and training are a much larger consideration than the participation of institutions of higher education in such programs. It is the latter type to which attention is here directed.

The direct Federal operation of college, university, or other educational programs, such as the service academies, postgraduate colleges, specialized schools such as Gallaudet College (for the deaf), and many types of programs of adult education are important evidences of Federal interest and activity in higher education. In these instances, however, the federally sponsored programs become but a part of the general structure of higher education in the United States.

Some Federal programs concentrate upon furthering the education of individuals or defined groups of individuals through providing direct financial assistance to those persons in loans, fellowships, or other forms of subvention. The individuals enroll in the institution as do any other students and take courses provided to all students. The sponsoring agency may or may not have a formal agreement with the institution for the educational services provided. This type of program, while obviously serving an educational or training purpose, is considered to be a program of student financial assistance. These programs, taken as a whole, are the largest of the Federal programs in numbers of persons involved. They include the veterans' educational benefits and the extensive programs for the upgrading of Government employees, both civilian and military. The primary effect upon institutions of higher education of such programs is simply to swell the number of students who enroll in their normal educational programs.

A type of program more difficult to classify is fellowships and trainee-ships. In some of these programs the principal recipient of Federal funds is the individual, although the programs frequently carry a cost-of-education grant to the institution. The primary purpose of these grants, however, is to increase trained manpower in designated fields and, hence, they are classified as a form of financial assistance to students.

Research assistantships made available to students through research contracts and grants are another form of subvention of the education and training of students. The primary objective of the Federal agency is to stimulate research, and, hence, these programs are classified as research programs.

Omitted from this discussion also are the extensive education and training programs designed primarily through agencies of the Department of State to cooperate with other countries in the educational and technical development of their resources. These programs include contracts with colleges and universities for assistance to programs in other countries, and extensive exchange-type programs in which students and faculty members from other countries and our own participate. The Department of Defense also contracts with institutions of higher education for the operation of overseas educational programs for armed service personnel and their families. Programs in which scientists, technicians, and professional workers are enabled to attend and participate in important international symposia and conferences and to collaborate in projects involving their colleagues in other countries are also an important educational activity classified here as international. Also some Federal agencies and departments provide funds to units of state governments which then sponsor programs in colleges and universities for the training of designated personnel for purposes pertinent to their missions. Such indirectly supported programs are also not included.

Finally, Federal agencies and departments are, in some instances, centers of education and training of college and university personnel in specialized fields.

Federally sponsored programs of education and training, in addition to those mentioned, range in their objectives throughout all levels of the educational system. They include programs for the strengthening of instruction in specified fields from elementary school subjects to postdoctorate studies; they support improvement of teaching and the content of the subject matter; they support the dissemination of knowledge from laboratories and libraries of the campus to individuals and groups of individuals in certain occupational fields; they train new personnel and retrain existing personnel in designated fields. They stimulate further learning by teachers in addition to that of their students.

A listing of the educational programs would include:

1. A variety of programs sponsored by the *National Science Foundation* designed to stimulate improvement in and strengthen education in the sciences. The programs include institutes and conferences held at colleges and universities during the academic year, summer session, or in shorter terms for teachers in elementary, secondary, or college teachers, respectively; projects for the improvement of course content, and instructional and library materials in the sciences; conferences on special science topics for college and university faculty members; research participation programs for well-qualified science students in high schools and colleges; and other types of educational experiences designed to stimulate interest and to further competence in scientific studies.

2. The *Department of Health, Education, and Welfare* administers a wide range of education and training programs, probably the broadest in scope and variety of any department of the Federal Government.

Under special provisions of the National Defense Education Act of 1958, the Office of Education arranges with colleges and universities for institutes in the modern foreign languages for teachers in elementary and secondary schools, and for institutes designed to increase the number and strengthen the quality of counselors and guidance specialists in the nation's schools. Selected institutions are also utilized as centers for the preparation of teachers and the development of instructional materials in a small number of foreign languages for which there is critical need in the national interest.

The Office of Vocational Rehabilitation shares with colleges and universities the costs of programs which train personnel needed in the rehabilitation of disabled persons. These programs cover the training of a broad range of specialists in social work, psychology, speech therapy, and related medical and nursing fields.

The Public Health Service, throughout its institutes and divisions, but principally in its National Institutes of Health, has large training programs in which grants are made to institutions of higher education for programs in which the objective is to increase the number and improve the quality of research workers, teachers, clinicians, and nurses in major medical and health fields. These training programs range from undergraduate to postgraduate levels, including career physicians, medical specialists, and public health personnel.

3. The *Atomic Energy Commission* sponsors summer institutes at selected institutions for faculty members of colleges and universities who wish to get specialized information and training in nuclear science, health physics, industrial hygiene, and other related fields. Some of this activity is carried on in cooperation with the National Science Foundation.

4. The *Department of Defense,* in addition to sponsoring programs of job-related training of military and civilian personnel, utilizes institutions of higher education in the operation of: (*a*) ROTC programs for the training of future officers of the armed services; (*b*) overseas educational centers near military bases in foreign countries for the continuing education of enlisted and officer personnel; and (*c*) the United States Armed Forces Institute, which brings opportunities to servicemen for off-duty educational advancement through correspondence study, at high school and college levels.

5. The *Department of Commerce* shares the cost of operating maritime schools for the training of merchant marines in several states.

6. The *Department of Agriculture,* through its Cooperative Extension Service, administers a nation-wide program of education and training. This program is administered in cooperation with every state and its counties, and includes a broad set of educational services designed to improve rural life through demonstrations, conferences, and the dissemination of information in the fields of agriculture and home economics. These programs feature public service programs for both youth and adults. The land-grant colleges are the vehicles for these activities.

7. The *Office of Education* administers the general appropriations provided for instructional purposes to land-grant colleges. This is primarily a fiscal operation, the allocation of funds being determined by legislative formula.

8. The *Department of State,* as already mentioned, involves colleges

in programs of training nationals of other countries, both in American institutions and in foreign countries, in fields of engineering, agriculture, economics, business administration, education, and many other fields. These programs resemble in pattern and purpose the agricultural extension services previously described.

Federal programs are dynamic and changing. Descriptions which fit a given year may be inaccurate or incomplete the next. Persons seeking to be currently informed can do no better than to keep in touch with the appropriate offices of the agencies or departments.

## Patterns of Distribution of Federal Programs and Funds

Estimates of the Federal funds expended in education and training programs of these types are reported in a recent bulletin of the Office of Education, *Federal Funds for Education: Fields, Levels, Recipients, 1959 and 1960.*[1] Significant aspects of this report for the purposes of the present discussion are that programs in the fields of agriculture, health, and service exceed in volume of funds the programs which are strictly military or defense-related; that the programs range across all major divisions of the curriculum, although concentrated on the physical and biological sciences; and that the focal point of the recently developed programs is at the level of graduate and professional education.

The nature of the Federal program in large measure predetermines the types of institutions that participate in it. Emphasis upon high-level specialization dictates the rise of colleges and universities which have strong graduate and professional programs. Emphasis upon scientific advance and technology dictates the use of institutions that have strong colleges of engineering, medicine, or agriculture, and their supporting basic sciences. The extensive experience of land-grant colleges in public service functions and the economic, technical, and educational development of their regions makes them a continuing resource which has been developed and widely used in federally sponsored programs of many types. In other instances, the location of Federal centers of

---

[1] Penrose B. Jackson and Dolores A. Steinhilber, Office of Education Circular 679 (Washington: Government Printing Office, 1962), 82 pp.

research or other Federal installations is a predisposing factor in the utilization of nearby colleges or universities.

Federal funds for the programs, therefore, tend to be concentrated in the strong and comparatively affluent universities that annually confer many doctorate-level degrees. The number of institutions participating in Federal programs of education and training is considerably larger than those involved in research programs, because of the larger use of undergraduate colleges in programs of science education and the involvement of all land-grant colleges in the agricultural programs.

In 1959, more than 450 institutions participated in one or more of the Federal programs of education and training here discussed. This number has been growing. The programs of the National Science Foundation involved the largest number—more than 385 institutions, both graduate and undergraduate. Next in order were the National Institutes of Health, involving approximately 150, and the Office of Education, nearly 125. (The education and training programs of the Department of Defense are the largest in number of persons trained and the volume of funds expended in the training. As explained earlier, many of these programs have been classified in this discussion as programs of assistance to students.)

About 84 percent of all Federal funds expended for these types of programs in colleges and universities in 1959 were allocated to 101 colleges and universities, 44 percent to 25 institutions, and 65 percent to 50 institutions. This degree of concentration results primarily from several circumstances built in to this type of analysis. First, a large part of the funds is taken by the agricultural programs which are limited to the land-grant colleges of the fifty states. Second, the training grants of the Public Health Service are concentrated in, although they are not limited to, the 85 to 90 institutions which have schools of medicine or public health. Third, fewer than 175 institutions in the United States confer the Ph.D. degree, and large numbers of the 175 confer only a few doctoral degrees or in a limited number of fields.

Almost 170 privately sponsored and almost 90 state-supported undergraduate colleges were participants. Some of these institutions were among the 100 institutions receiving the largest amounts of Federal funds from an individual program. In general, these institutions are those that are recognized among their sister institutions as strong, prestigious institutions in which above-average quotas of their graduates continue on to graduate or professional studies. The list of institutions that have participated in these programs broadens with each year, since in some programs—institutes and conferences—a rotation procedure is used in locating these programs. Within the groups of participating undergraduate colleges, however, Federal funds tend also to be concentrated. For example, 25 private undergraduate colleges received 62 percent of the Federal funds allocated to all 88 institutions of their type that participated in 1959.

Thirty of 83 colleges attended predominantly by Negroes participated in federally sponsored programs of education and training, primarily through land-grant appropriations or by participation in institute-type programs.

In summary, federally sponsored programs of education and training taken as a whole are congeries of specialized interests seeking specialized educational outcomes. In the fields in which they operate, they add strength to the on-going purposes and programs of colleges and universities. They range widely but unevenly across the educational curricula both in level and field. Recently developed programs and proposals reflect (*a*) the national urgencies for the development of highly qualified manpower in many fields, (*b*) the transition from programs that primarily assist rural development to programs which also tackle the problems of urban life, and (*c*) the cultivation of greater competence and wisdom in the management of the nation's growing responsibilities in world affairs.

The participation of the Federal Government in these undertakings has, in general, been taken by the educational community as natural and necessary. The criticisms are more directed toward administrative procedure than toward purpose or policy. There are misgivings, however, about the piecemeal nature of Federal activity and strong protests against actions which would centralize the administration of Federal programs. There is vigilance against actions which threaten the independence and integrity of institutions and their traditional freedoms.

# FEDERAL PROGRAMS
# OF INTERNATIONAL EDUCATION

## H. Field Haviland, Jr.
DIRECTOR, FOREIGN POLICY STUDIES,
THE BROOKINGS INSTITUTION

O NE CAN SCARCELY RECALL THE TRANQUIL, PREWAR ERA WHEN THE globe-trotting academic was a rarity, and the Government was quite unconcerned whether professors ventured abroad or stayed home tending their gardens and campus politics. During the seething postwar years, however, no red-blooded professor stays in his own country if he can possibly wangle his passage abroad, and the Government has become a major entrepreneur in stimulating the growing world-wide traffic in students and teachers.

Cultural exchange is advancing from the wings to the center of the foreign policy stage. The United States Government has changed its attitude toward such activities from passive good will to active support. The focus has shifted substantially from the comfortable business of exchanging scholars with their counterparts in relatively developed and familiar countries to the more arduous task of assisting the advancement of relatively less developed and less familiar nations. President Kennedy enunciated the new cultural gospel when he said, a month after his inauguration, "There is no better way of helping the new nations of Latin America, Africa and Asia in their present pursuit of freedom and better living conditions than by assisting them to develop their human resources through education. Likewise there is no better way to strengthen our bonds of understanding and friendship with older nations than through educational and cultural exchange."

In examining current Federal programs of international education, I shall concentrate primarily on those of major significance to our institutions of higher learning. After describing briefly the relevant programs, I shall discuss in some detail the principal policy issues raised by these programs.

## Pattern of Existing Federal Programs

Federal international education programs comprise a heterogeneous and sometimes unruly flock of activities scattered among twenty-four Federal organizations, but only eight of these are considered to be of major significance. The Secretary of State, aided by an Assistant Secretary and Bureau for Educational and Cultural Affairs, is regarded by the President as the principal shepherd responsible for exercising primary leadership in persuading the members of the flock to move in more or less consistent directions. As is frequently the case with such arrangements, however, the other agencies are not always responsive to the advice of "Big Brother." The seven other units of major significance are: the Agency for International Development, the Department of Defense, the United States Information Agency, the National Science Foundation, the Department of Health, Education, and Welfare, the National Aeronautics and Space Administration, and the Peace Corps.

The *Department of State,* through its Bureau of International Educational and Cultural Affairs, conducts international exchange-of-persons programs, including American and foreign students, teachers, professors, leaders and specialists; encourages and assists the presentation abroad of American performing artists; provides assistance to American-sponsored educational institutions abroad; stimulates the establishment of chairs in American studies in foreign universities; encourages study and research abroad designed to increase American competence in foreign languages and areas; and is the principal link with the East-West Center in Hawaii.

The *Agency for International Development,* under its mutual security programs, brings foreign nationals of countries participating in technical cooperation and development grant activities to the United States or to third countries to engage in technical training, study, or observation. United States specialists are sent abroad to give technical assistance. AID is the principal agency concerned with helping the new nations develop their educational systems and human resources.

The *Department of Defense* is concerned primarily with the training of foreign military personnel in the United States and elsewhere under the Military Assistance Training Program. Other programs include scholarships, fellowships, training, and overseas research grants in scientific fields.

The *United States Information Agency* is primarily concerned with the international exchange of educational and cultural materials, information, and related activities. Overseas it serves as the main agency for the Department of State in handling educational and cultural exchanges and related activities. Our cultural attachés are on the United States Information Service staffs abroad.

The *National Science Foundation* sends fellows to study overseas; American scientists go abroad to conduct research and to attend foreign institutes; foreign scientists participate in NSF institutes and lecture at American universities.

*Department of Health, Education, and Welfare* international projects are carried on through its *National Institutes of Health*. Fellowships are awarded to Americans for training overseas; international postdoctoral fellowships are awarded to foreign scientists for training in the United States; and eminent foreign scientists are brought to NIH for temporary employment or research. The Office of Education supports international programs in American universities under the National Defense Education Act and conducts comparative studies of education in various countries. The Office also helps the Department of State handle teacher exchanges and visiting educators.

The *National Aeronautics and Space Administration,* through its international programs, enlists participation of scientists of other countries in increasing man's understanding and use of his spatial environment. Grants for foreign nationals include postdoctoral grants to scientists for research at NASA centers; technical training for technicians and scientists at NASA centers; fellowships to graduate students at United States universities; and visits from foreign officials and scientists for purposes of observation and consultation.

The *Peace Corps* arranges for the placement abroad of skilled American volunteers in developing nations to assist in filling the need for skilled manpower. The volunteers serve local institutions in teaching and training and in various types of work programs.

## Major Policy Issues

While this vast movement of people and ideas has carried the light of learning to all corners of the globe, there remain major problems. In this discussion, I shall concentrate primarily on those programs and issues that most directly and significantly concern institutions of higher learning, chiefly related to activities administered by the Department of State, including the AID.

### BASIC GOALS AND PROGRAMS

First, there is the question of deciding fundamentally where we want to go and how we intend to get there. Most recent studies of international cultural programs emphasize that relatively few universities have done an adequate job of determining their long-range commitment to international education and designing comprehensive programs to support that commitment. The recent report of the Ford Foundation–sponsored Committee on the University and World Affairs concludes that ". . . a critical examination of existing resources and gaps . . . would seem a logical first step, to be followed by detailed planning, school by school and department by department, of ways to fortify existing programs and create essential new ones."

The foundation for such planning must be a clear sense of how the interests of the university relate to its international involvement. The basic justification for such activity is simply an extension of the university's traditional role in helping to advance the cultural and material well-being of its constituent community. Just as the community served by the university has expanded domestically, so it is now expanding beyond the nation to other cultures and peoples whose welfare has become increasingly intertwined with our own. Internationally, as well as domestically, the university benefits by helping to strengthen the community on whose well-being its own survival and development are dependent.

Because resources are always limited, however, it is essential that each university carefully appraise its total long-range international objectives to be certain that its appetite is not beyond its means. This effort will be aided by establishing in each institution some kind of center for stimulating and facilitating long-range thinking about the problem and for developing comprehensive plans that will keep peace and harmony among the various colleges and departments concerned. There is also need for each university to improve its communication and cooperation with other interested institutions. This can be done through various channels, including professional associations such as the American Council on Education, governmentally sponsored advisory bodies, and the newly organized interuniversity Education and World Affairs.

If the university is to gird its loins adequately to do battle with the problems of the world, it will do well to give priority attention to strengthening its internal resources in certain fundamental respects. These might be summarized briefly as follows: (1) The entire curriculum, both undergraduate and graduate, should be given a complete examination to make certain that each academic muscle is pulling its appropriate weight in relation to the international objectives of the university. (2) Faculty members should be encouraged and supported in acquiring international background relevant to their teaching and research. (3) An international component should be required as an integral part of every student's undergraduate program. (4) Graduate schools should strengthen the international aspects of their offerings. (5) Specialized international programs, at both the undergraduate and graduate levels, should strive for a reasonable balance between area and functional approaches, building on elements of special strength and utilizing neighboring resources without attempting to cover all subjects. (6) Training recalcitrant American tongues to speak other languages is an essential ingredient of any comprehensive international strategy. (7) Increased opportunities for overseas training and research should be afforded both students and faculty. (8) The university should play a leading role in helping to improve international educational training at the primary and secondary levels and in adult programs.

### DEVELOPMENT ASSISTANCE

Probably the greatest challenge that has helped catapult the university into international orbit is the rapid postwar emergence of the developing countries. This is the most radically novel element in the overseas involvement of the university. It is generating the greatest overseas demand for university talent and is responsible for the largest proportion of Federal support for international educational activities. Thus the problems associated with development programs are among the most significant issues confronting the university.

Academic participation in federally supported aid programs takes two major forms: (*a*) sending American specialists overseas, either as employees of a university under a Government contract or as direct employees of the Government, and (*b*) receiving foreign nationals in American universities for training related to overseas development programs.

One basic issue raised by these activities has to do with the scope and depth of university involvement in collaborating with the Government to design broad strategies of national and regional development. The approach has been for university participation to be rather narrowly limited to administering highly specialized projects for killing more mosquitoes or growing more rice. The Government and the universities have been guilty of failing to look at the whole elephant, failing to develop adequate concepts, skills, and procedures to design and implement comprehensive, integrated development strategies. To help meet this need, the universities should give greater attention to cultivating both doctrines and personnel concerned with general educational development planning. Prying open minds that have been closed for centuries to admit new facts, new values, and new ways of thinking lies at the heart of the development process. There is greater need than ever for people who have the motivation, ideas, and techniques to design and execute broad, long-range strategies of educational development related to general economic, social, and political advancement. The universities have a special responsibility and capability to meet this need, drawing on the resources not only of schools of education but other relevant fields.

Philip Coombs, former Assistant Secretary of State for Educational and Cultural Affairs, has said, "The same daring and ingenuity—the same research and development approach—which our educational institutions have helped to create and apply so fruitfully to such other fields as agriculture, industry, and communications, must now be applied to education itself."

*Government contracts.*—The principal governmental resources provided to support university participation in overseas development programs are governed by the device of the Government contract which makes the university, rather than an individual, the Government's agent. As of June 30, 1962, the Government had in force 107 contracts totaling $109 million with 88 universities operating in 37 countries. This massive program, which had no comparable counterpart before the Second World War, has engineered a radically new injection of the university into the development of the emerging countries. Despite considerable growing pains and an occasional acute case of the bends, these programs have made an invaluable net contribution to both the contracting universities and to the developing countries. Yet several recent studies of these operations have suggested that the contract program still suffers from difficulties that hamper its effectiveness.

One problem rises out of the old dilemma of trying to force a square peg into a round hole. A university is sometimes asked to perform functions that are not suitable either to universities generally or to a particular institution. Both the Government and the universities have an obligation to consider carefully whether a given institution has the basic motivation and capacity to do a particular job successfully. A critical consideration is the availability of qualified personnel. Although a university seldom has a complete assortment of all the types needed to staff an operation during the entire period of the contract, an institution should have a strong core of its own faculty capable of guiding the project and should not be a mere "hiring hall" to recruit personnel from outside the contracting university. One device that should be experimented with more fully is the establishment of associations or consortia of universities and colleges to facilitate the pooling of resources in support of contract operations.

Another difficulty has to do with working out a satisfactory understanding among all the parties concerned, particularly the university, the Government, and the host country. Although the harmonizing of these several interests depends on many factors, including the refractory nature of some human beings, the process would be greatly aided by bringing the university into the negotiations at an earlier stage than has been usual. This would give the university a more adequate opportunity to help draw the blueprint and to appraise its own capacity to help build the structure.

In line with my earlier comment about the need for broader educational planning, the contract device could and should be used more than it is at present to encourage and support the universities in designing and executing comprehensive educational development programs. The universities are potentially, if not always currently, peculiarly well suited to fill this need.

Still another problem is the extent to which the Government should be expected to contribute a "quid" in return for the university's "quo."

It is only enlightened self-interest on the part of the Government to provide at least part of the cost of teaching materials and research related to projects in order to strengthen the motivation and capacity of the faculty to service such projects. It is also desirable for the Government to do everything possible, through policy declarations, financial support, and administrative arrangements, to reinforce the long-range nature of the university's participation in contract operations. The relatively bobtailed emphasis of the past has made it difficult for universities to become seriously committed to such operations and to mobilize adequate resources, especially able personnel, to fulfill their obligations.

Government support should also be given to supplementary activities that would enhance the effectiveness of such operations. There is need for more adequate general orientation of university personnel going overseas in order to prepare them to work in a particular cultural setting, including intensive language preparation. And more systematic evaluation of some, if not all, such missions would provide a better basis for appraising the past and improving the future.

Finally, the Government should continue to be urged to loosen the strait jacket of governmental financial and administrative regulations. Some controls are legitimate and necessary, but there is still evidence that existing practices hobble the universities far more than they need or ought to for effective operation.

*Direct Government employment.*—It is also important to keep in mind the university's role in relation to those persons who work directly for the Government on development projects. The Agency for International Development alone directly employs about 15,000 persons, of whom about 13,000 serve abroad. The university is not their employer, but it can make a major contribution in helping to train, recruit, and maintain able staffs for such operations.

In support of this effort, there is need for the universities to improve their collaboration with the Government in assessing the Government's long-range personnel needs for development operations, designing educational programs to help meet these requirements, supporting the improvement of governmental career opportunities, and encouraging able people to choose such careers. These endeavors would be further aided by facilitating short-term governmental service for university faculty members to savor Washington and short-term leaves to enable governmental employees to take advantage of opportunities on campuses to enlarge their knowledge and understanding.

*Foreign scholars in the United States.*—The other major aspect of university involvement in development activities is the large and growing flow of foreign scholars to United States institutions for training, research, and teaching. During the academic year 1961–62, 58,000 foreign students from 149 countries enrolled in 1,700 institutions of higher learning in the United States. Of these, approximately 75 percent came from the developing countries. A little more than 9 percent of all visiting foreign students reported United States grants as their source of support. In addition, 5,530 professors, instructors, lecturers, and advanced research scholars from 90 countries were on academic assignment at 390 United States colleges and universities. Approximately 55 percent of these were from the developing countries.

Of these visiting scholars, approximately 7,000 were brought to the United States by the Agency for International Development as participant-trainees related to AID-sponsored development programs overseas. As many as one-third of these went to university campuses for at least one semester.

This remarkable influx of scholars, which has been increasing at the prodigious rate of 10 percent a year for the last decade, presents United States universities with an extraordinary opportunity to strengthen knowledge and understanding across the globe. The fact that more foreign scholars want to come to the United States than to any other country, despite the availability of some juicier fellowships in certain other countries, including the Soviet Union and Communist China, testifies to the general satisfaction of our intellectual customers. At the same time, it is clear to all who have observed these programs that much more could and should be done to improve the experiences of visiting scholars.

One problem has to do with the level, numbers, and periods of time spent in the country. In view of the swelling flood of United States students seeking admission to our campuses, there is some consternation about the rising tide of foreign students, which may reach the level of 125,000 a year by 1970.

In thinking about this problem, it should be kept in mind that foreign students comprise less than 1 percent of the student population on most campuses. In only nine universities does the foreign segment account for as much as 5 percent of the student body. Nonetheless, the universities and the Government should cooperate in making certain that, in fairness to both the American community and to other nations, scholars admitted from overseas have the intellectual capacity, personal qualities, cultural conditioning, and material support necessary to make their educational experiences successful. The Government has already taken modest steps to assist in this effort and should be encouraged to do more.

As for the level of educational visitors, experience suggests that the United States may make a greater relative contribution to cultural development by encouraging visits of scholars at the graduate and postgraduate levels than at the undergraduate level. The length of stay must be determined by the requirements of each educational program, keeping in mind the desirability of sharing such opportunities widely but avoiding the encouragement of perennial students.

A crucial aspect of the visiting scholar program is the counseling, selection, placement, and orientation phase prior to the student's arrival at the host university. One of the weaknesses in the present process is the absence of adequate standards, personnel, and procedures abroad. The African Student Program of American Universities, administered in collaboration with the African-American Institute, has pioneered an improved selection program for African students. Much more needs to be done, however, not only in Africa but in other areas, to advise scholars, select them, recommend their placement, and prepare them culturally for their visit. This should be done not only by strengthening United States Government staffs abroad but also by developing private resources that can assist in such matters.

The preparatory process overseas needs to be matched by more adequate general orientation, counseling, and English language training in the United States. Despite substantial progress, such as the development of the role of the foreign student adviser, further improvement is needed, including increased governmental support for such activities.

As for the academic program to be pursued by the visitor, the special conditions of other countries often raise the question of the degree to which our university offerings should be revised to accommodate the foreign national. In many cases, fortunately, present offerings are sufficiently relevant so that no significant adjustment is required. The most frequent need for special treatment is in cultural and language orientation rather than the scholar's primary field. In some cases, however, special conditions, particularly with regard to the developing countries, warrant designing distinct programs for the foreign scholar.

Then there is the problem of financial support. While the Federal Government is devoting greater resources than ever before to international educational programs, there is still a tendency, especially in Congress, to be more parsimonious in this field than in the more strictly propagandistic efforts of the United States Information Agency or the educational activities of the military. Educational exchange programs in Latin America and Africa are especially threadbare because of the lack of foreign currencies as well as dollar funds. The Government and the universities need to collaborate to ensure that adequate financial resources are made available to support their international educational programs. This effort should include improving employment opportunities for foreign scholars.

Finally, there is the need to reinforce the follow-up process after the scholar has returned home. More should be done to strengthen continuing contact with those who have completed educational experiences in the United States. Suitable steps should be taken to assist such scholars to find appropriate career opportunities, and more systematic efforts should be made to evaluate these programs as a basis for improving them.

#### EXPORT OF UNITED STATES SCHOLARS

In addition to the activities designed to assist the development of the emerging countries, largely under the aegis of the Agency for International Development, there are governmental programs that support the exposure of United States scholars in all fields to all countries, both developed and underdeveloped nations. The principal effort of this nature is conducted under the new Fulbright-Hays Act passed in 1961. This program makes it possible for approximately 2,000 American graduate students and postdoctoral scholars to go abroad each year. Since the trail-blazing Fulbright Act was passed in 1946, this program has enabled approximately 18,000 Americans to go overseas, and thus strengthened United States intellectual bonds with other peoples and enriched our own culture. Still the program suffers from several deficiencies.

One need is for better long-range planning in close collaboration with related public and private agencies, including the universities. Such planning should seek to overcome present gaps in the program, such as the weakness of the program in Africa and Latin America, due to past reliance on the fortuitous availability of local currencies. Also important are the interests of the participating United States institutions and individuals, including their desire to foster research, as well as the interests of the host countries.

Another problem is to maintain high standards of selection. As the focus has shifted toward the developing countries, where conditions are often arduous and financial support meager, it has been difficult to find qualified personnel for all the openings. Selection requires more recruiting effort, more adequate financing (especially transportation for dependents), and more effective procedures for evaluating candidates.

Other steps need to be taken to ensure that those granted fellowships have effective experiences overseas. More adequate planning, including better communication between the host institutions abroad and the private as well as public administering agencies in this country, will help to match the man to the opening more effectively. Most American participants need better orientation than is now provided. Finally, more effective follow-up and evaluation are needed to help the returned grantee make the most of his experience and to distill from these efforts lessons for the future.

## Conclusion

As we come to the end of this quick Cook's tour of some of the major programs and problems associated with Federal international educational activities, it is useful to glance back briefly over the ground we have covered in order to have clearly in mind the high points that dominate the landscape. The most striking phenomenon that emerges from the postwar experience is that both the developed and underdeveloped countries have come increasingly to recognize that education can and should be a central instrument, not just a fifth wheel, for the conscious and fundamental transformation of world society.

The most severe international test facing our overseas educational efforts is how to nourish the progress of the developing countries without squandering scarce resources and without encouraging richer tastes than can be satisfied with the means available. This task calls for the most radical revision of old concepts, methods, and institutions and for an extraordinary mobilization of human and material resources. At the same time, there remains the related, more familiar, and still important function of encouraging general educational cooperation in all fields and all countries. Both of these enterprises are in our interest and can be mutually reinforcing.

These efforts have pressed the university and the Government into each other's arms to a degree never foreseen before the Second World War. Although they have been able to resolve many of their differences, one has the feeling that, as in the case of some other alliances, neither partner has taken a sufficiently long-range or broad view of the relationship, and neither has developed an adequate definition of its own interests or effectively reconciled its interests with those of the other. The Government wants university assistance in pursuing certain economic, social, and political goals but is reluctant to be very permissive with either its purse strings or its apron strings. The university wants Government support for the domestic as well as overseas aspects of its international involvement, but chafes at limitations imposed by confining regulations and parsimonious budgets. Perhaps the best advice one can give these partners for the future is to urge them to work more systematically and cooperatively to identify and harmonize their long-range interests and requirements regarding international education, keeping in mind their obligations to their domestic as well as their overseas constituencies.

# OF WINDS AND WINDMILLS:
# FREE UNIVERSITIES AND PUBLIC POLICY

## McGeorge Bundy

SPECIAL ASSISTANT TO THE PRESIDENT
OF THE UNITED STATES

M Y GENERAL PURPOSE IS TO OFFER A FEW COMMENTS FROM A MIDDLE
position on the great issues that are the subject of this meeting.
I am not in the daily stream of these matters now, but I do have lively
memories of many years of concern for this issue as it appears to a university administrator, and for nearly two years now I have been learning to think in the terms that are habitual to residents of Washington.
So against my present irresponsibility, I may perhaps set the advantage
of some experience of the general feelings which are normal at both
ends of the line. In doing so, I should like to impose on your generosity
and speak as if I were still an academic administrator—of *our* problems
and opportunities, not *yours.*

From this position, I would like to suggest that it is time to separate
the propositions which are certain from those which are still under
legitimate study and discussion. My own conviction is that the experience of the last fifteen years has demonstrated beyond serious question
the validity of several highly important propositions about which doubt
was widespread at the end of the Second War. At the same time,
and in part as a direct result of the successes we have had, new questions have been proposed and they are in urgent need of sharp definition and quick resolution. It is a time, then, for clear understanding of
what we have learned and prompt attack upon the issues which remain
to be settled. It is a first step in this process that we should separate
the one from the other.

## Federal Dollars and Institutional Freedom

Of the propositions which, in my judgment, have been demonstrated
beyond doubt, two are of high importance. The first is that Federal

investment in the higher learning has been extraordinarily productive, both for the national security and for the quality of our civilization. The second is that the processes of this investment have, on the whole, been such as to enhance the freedom and independent strength of American colleges and universities.

The productivity of Federal investment in higher education is probably a notion that needs little demonstration in this audience. Whether we consider the principal immediate objectives of advancing the nation's defense and improving the nation's health, or the wider issue of the quality and quantity of American science, we can say quite frankly that without the Federal Government our present levels of achievement would be impossible. This proposition is self-evident to responsible scientists, responsible university administrators, responsible Government officials, and responsible members of leading committees of Congress. Its self-evidence is the primary cause of the very rapid curve of growth in Federal support for science and technology. Within this proposition there can be many questions and reservations, but its essential and sweeping validity is clear.

The second proposition is equally plain, at least in my judgment, but I recognize that it needs more argument. We are so accustomed to a nervous suspicion of "Federal control" that it is not easy to accept the notion that the Federal dollar may in fact be a reinforcement of freedom. So let us look at the facts.

Let me at once recognize that the general proposition is subject to substantial reservations and qualifications. There are many, and there is no better way to become acquainted with them than to serve as dean at a place like Harvard where the faculty has a cantankerous habit of independence. I know about the problem of project support, the problem of paper work, the problem of the undersupported field of inquiry, the problem of badly designed fellowship or loan programs, the problem of oaths and affidavits, and, above all, the problem of the internal hemorrhage which can be created by Federal money which does not meet overhead costs. These are all real problems, and unless he has changed since I used to work for him, President Pusey will have said some sharp things about them earlier today.

But all these weaknesses can be repaired, and progress is being made on most of them. And neither singly nor in combination do they outbalance the overwhelming positive effects of Federal money. I will say flatly that American higher learning is more and not less free and strong because of Federal funds.

There are a number of ways of demonstrating this proposition, but I content myself with three. The first is quite simple: it is that freedom is the opportunity to act as well as the absence of restraint. Without Federal money, our scientists would not have been free, in the most precise sense of the word, to do what they have done in the last fifteen years. It is no good to talk about academic freedom when antiquated laboratories, inadequate instruments, and overcrowded teaching schedules make serious inquiry impossible. When it is not given under crippling limitations and restrictions, money is quite simply an instrument of freedom, in the universities as elsewhere in life. This is a point so obvious that we frequently forget it.

My second supporting argument is comparative in form. My claim is simply that nearly all the money which supports higher education in this country carries with it some risk of limitation upon the freedom of academic life, and that the record of the Federal dollar does not suffer by comparison with any other major source of funds.

All of us know that the national academic budget, on the income side, is a many-colored mixture of funds from a wide variety of sources: from tuition, from legislative appropriations, from annual gifts, from endowments, from contracts, from foundations, from Government, from alumni, from church and state, from industry and individuals. We also know, although we don't always admit it, that almost every one of these sources of funds carries with it the hazard that it may limit our freedom of action. It is a standard pleasantry in our private gatherings that members of public universities should speak in envious tones to their colleagues in private colleges of the beauty of life without a state legislature to placate, and when this joke is trotted out, the man from the private college is likely to reply by offering to match his five most critical alumni against any legislative committee in the country. All of us here know that suspicion of the principles of academic freedom is endemic among legislatures and alumni. It is endemic—seldom dominant, but always present—and the freedom of American higher learning as a whole cannot be measured by the unusual independence of action of a few colleges and universities with strong traditions.

Even when we leave aside the cruder forms of attack upon freedom of inquiry, there is little reason to single out the Federal dollar for criticism. An unbalanced allocation of resources is more characteristic of alumni than of Government agencies, and the overadministered grant was invented by the large private foundations long before the Government became a significant force in academic life. Indeed, my own experience as an academic administrator leads me to the view that on balance the Federal Government makes its grants and signs its contracts with a better perception of the real needs of the higher learning than one can find, on the average, in the major private foundations.

When we look at the over-all pattern of higher education, the record of the Federal dollar is still less open to comparative attack. The Federal dollar has not been used, as state dollars have been, to support whole departments and majors in subjects that do not belong at the college or university level. The Federal dollar has not been used, as private gifts have been, for overly luxurious athletic facilities that are reminiscent more of the country club than of the academy. The Federal dollar has not been used for the subsidy of athletes or the construction of pretentious and egocentric memorial buildings. In the best of our institutions, the Federal dollar has been, on the average, as good as any other—always excepting the wholly unrestricted gift. In American academic life as a whole, the qualitative rating of Federal money would, in my considered conviction, be better than that of any other major class of income.

My third claim for the quality of Federal money is that the decisions by which it is allocated are made by processes more nearly fitted to the great tradition of academic life than is the case with any other major source of funds. Within the broad lines of authorizations laid down by statute, what governs the decisions of the Federal Government on the whole is the collective judgment of outstanding members of the academic community itself. Statutory provisions may not be perfect, but the Congress has encouraged intelligent administrative interpretation, and, in practice, the qualitative performance of Federal money has been set by the judgment and taste of Federal administrators in seeking and using the counsel of qualified academic men. On balance that judgment has been excellent.

I emphasize this point because it is one of cardinal importance for the future of relations between Government and universities. The greatest single safeguard for this relationship is the interplay of thought and decision of large numbers of individuals with proper professional qualifications on both sides of the line. This principle is embodied historically in the statute which established the National Academy of Sciences. It was followed in practice during the extraordinary events of the Second World War, when the Federal Government and the academic community first worked at full pressure together. This is a meeting of academic administrators and, as a former member of that club, I recognize and even share the feeling many of you must have that real wisdom and judgment in academic budgeting belongs to the president, or at least to the dean.

The institution in which I myself was an administrator has a tradition of quite high-handed and centralized executive behavior—and it has not suffered, on balance, as a consequence. Yet the fact is, and we all know this too, that executive energy in academic administration always depends for its effectiveness on a most intensive process of consultation and consensus. Our colleges and universities serve best when they serve in their own way, under processes that meet their own requirements. The most serious mistake a lay granting body can make is to try to decide for itself how a given objective can be met by academic institutions. In some statutory provisions and in some administrative practices the Federal Government has certainly made this mistake, but—again on balance—its major granting agencies have followed a very different and much more constructive course.

## Affirmation of a Constructive Partnership

Assuming that you are not in violent revolt against the argument so far, we now have two propositions: first, Federal money has repaid its cost production in most important ways; second, it has been a reinforcement of the freedom of the higher learning. From these conclusions it should follow that the traditional fear and hostility to Federal aid to higher education would be abandoned, and certainly there has been some progress in this direction. The anguished prophecies of earlier decades are heard less often—and from less respectable sources. One incidental benefit has been that representatives of private colleges, as their annual accounts begin to show large admixtures of Federal money, have somewhat muted the warnings against the "low standards" and "political pressure of public institutions" with which they have too often sought to attract private funds.

But much remains to be done. Too much of our time is still spent in arguing a case which, at least among ourselves, we should have learned to take for granted. Too many of us are acting still as if Federal participation in the higher learning were still an uncertain experiment, instead of the stable and growing reality which it is. And this is what I mean by my somewhat foolish title: generalized hostility to Federal money is as senseless as tilting at a windmill. The windmill is here to stay, and it is no man's enemy. Indeed, this whole business of Federal money in higher education represents a constructive partnership which benefits both sides—and I will press my title just a bit further—to suggest that the analogy of the windmill can be applied in two quite contrasting ways, both of them fitting to the case.

A windmill, as you know, and as Don Quixote did not, is a peaceful agency for making wind do work. The wind may blow from many directions, but a well-designed windmill gets results in terms of the grain that is ground. So it is with a well-designed university. It exists to advance learning, and the winds of financial support—whatever their course—are caught and turned to the university's purpose. So it is also with a soundly conceived program of Federal aid: such a program also can be seen as a windmill, in which the university's "winnowing breezes" provide the force that serves the program's purpose. The analogies are labored, I fear, but in this clumsy way they both hold true. This is what has been demonstrated conclusively in the last twenty years, and this is what we must take for granted as we examine the real issues of the present and future.

But what we take for granted we should also never fail to preach. Nothing is plainer about the partnership between Government and the higher learning than the simple fact that most Americans are deeply unaware of it. That is not a healthy situation, for over the long run we will not, as citizens, support with taxes what we do not understand. This is not the place for a study of the unusual pattern of circumstance which has produced the curious present situation—there is nothing discreditable about it—nor has it been done in any secretive way. The people's representatives in Congress have followed the whole process closely, and for those who *have* followed it closely this has been a fine example of responsible government in action.

But the ordinary citizen really has not followed it at all, and in the universities and colleges we have not done nearly enough to tell him about it. This is a mistake, for in the American governmental process it is the immediate beneficiary of Federal activity whose job it is to assure public understanding that the benefits he receives are in the public interest. It is not enough to persuade ourselves, in private discussion, that the help we get is deeply in the public interest. The taxpayer deserves explanation, acknowledgment, and thanks. He has every right to an understanding pride in the degree to which he is himself a partner in one of the most productive and effective activities in all our great society, and if he does not feel that pride, the fault is ours.

## Higher Education's Responsibilities in the Relationship

The partnership exists; it is productive; it needs our energetic and continuous defense. So far so good. But what can we do to improve it? Each of us, I am sure, can think of a dozen immediate and concrete answers to that question—but let me offer instead a few more general comments.

First, I think we need to give constant attention to all the multiplicity of details which affect our relationship. It is all well and good to make sweeping statements such as those I have already offered, but these statements stand or fall on what is actually done in a hundred different programs. The Government, most fortunately, presents not one but many faces to the university world, and if at any given moment the best face is very beautiful, the worst is likely to be quite a mess—and it may even have effects like those of Medusa. Law by law, program by program, office by office, and even case by case we must ourselves police the partnership. I have already indicated my belief that a critically important role in these matters belongs to the qualified scholars in each relevant field, but you who are responsible to the wider public, as heads of institutions, cannot safely leave this labor to your scholars alone.

The same hazards and necessities which justify alert and active central administration within our universities demand your attention in the relation between your institution and the Government: cliques can form in the process of counsel to Washington as readily as in a closed and self-satisfied university department. And the intrusion of unhealthy influence from the donor is not always resisted by professors with special interests; like bad alumni and misguided legislatures, Washington bureaucrats require the vigilance of administrations as well as faculties. I well remember myself, from my years at Harvard, how often along the battleground of negotiation with Government agencies it was the quite unscholarly administrative officer in charge of contracts, and not the high-minded and learned professor in search of funds, who maintained the true principles of academic autonomy. And on the rare, but real, occasion in which Federal assistance becomes excessively generous, it is unfortunately very unlikely that the immediate beneficiaries will complain. Someone else should, and I think administrators are nominated.

Our responsibility is still more clear in a second field: the prevention—or repair—of imbalances in American learning which may be created, quite unintentionally, by Federal programs. I am not an alarmist on this point—there are very learned men whom I hold in great affection who seem to me just plain wrong in their fear of the rise of science. Nevertheless, it seems certain to me that the general welfare does require us to be watchful against distortions. And my own conviction is that the best single remedy is to seek for ways of gradually expanding the flow of Federal money so that it works for the reinforcement of the higher learning as a whole. This can be done, I believe, without any loss of effectiveness in meeting the particular and legitimately urgent purposes which have inspired existing programs. But we will have to help.

To do this job and others, I believe, we will have to show, individually and collectively, a new level of attention to this whole problem. So my third recommendation is that we must do much more, in the future, in our Washington work. Until now, you know, the Federal dollar has been badly underprivileged in its share of attention from high-level academic administrators. To put it quite bluntly, most of us have simply let the money roll in, contenting ourselves from time to time with well-bred complaints about bureaucrats or less well-bred sneers when too much money seemed to be going to someone else. We are beginning to do better, but there is a lot still to be done.

Last month, in a most unfortunate vote which has hurt the whole country, a sensible and careful compromise bill for the support of higher education was defeated in the House of Representatives. Many forces combined to defeat that bill, and I am convinced that many of those who voted against it had not had a proper chance to study what they are doing. But what I want to emphasize here is that higher education itself was badly outlobbied on its own bill by forces that had, by comparison, only a marginal interest in the matter. As a result, laboratories will not get built, students in need will not get help, and libraries will remain on the drawing board. Our case is good—but we have not worked hard enough for it.

In all this there is one habit we must learn to beat—the habit of acting alone. No trade association or labor organization or farm group or medical association would dream of advancing on Washington in the genial and undisciplined confusion of individual approaches which we employ by habit. In part, of course, that is because all these other groups are so much less competitive than we are. People who talk about the rigors of competition in business have never watched us in our efforts to land a big grant or a big professor or a big philanthropist. We have got to learn to be less cutthroat, at least in our efforts with the Federal Government, as a whole. But it is not just a matter of avoiding competition—it is one of developing effective and operative concern for the higher learning as a whole. We who are administrators in American colleges and universities today have allowed ourselves to be oppressed, by a thousand forces, into a brutal struggle for the survival and reinforcement of our own individual institutions. Each of us is so deeply engaged in this lonely process that we have not learned how to combine in the common interest. Indeed we have been wary of organization, suspicious of one another, and unable, from our different preoccupations, to give adequate outward voice to our overwhelming common interest.

I am not telling you anything you do not know, I am sure—and I recognize that much has been done, since I had active knowledge of these matters, to strengthen academic organization and representation in Washington. I even know a little at first hand of Logan Wilson's own outstanding efforts. But I do not think it's wrong—or that Mr. Wilson will disagree—to emphasize again that the job of presenting and re-presenting the case for higher education simply does not and will not do itself. *We* have to do it—and we have not done it as we should.

## *Higher Education's Responsibility to the Nation*

That brings me to my last and most important point. The case for higher education—and for its partnership with the Federal Government—is not merely a matter of our common interest in technical progress, or in the national defense, or in medical research. It is not merely a matter of the evident need for improved facilities, the obligation to open doors for young people, or the honorable race for space. It is not even a matter merely of the health and strength of the higher learning as a whole. What is going on here is a great adventure in the purpose and performance of a free people. We have built great private institutions, small and large. We have developed magnificent state universities, and we are going to have more of them.

In the last twenty years it has become plain that this whole vast enterprise requires—and is required for—the interest of the nation as a whole. This is a cause for care, and for attention to detail, for new organization and effort, for explanation and for advocacy. But it is also a cause for pride and hope. For what has been accomplished so far proves beyond doubt that there is good for all America in this new partnership. Surely it is our responsibility—our urgent duty—to see that what is done continues to be good and gets better; that what needs to be done receives more and wider understanding; and that the larger meaning of this high achievement of our Federal democracy is understood and recognized. This great chapter of accomplishment, properly understood and properly sustained, can be a major reinforcement to our whole society as a demonstration of effective action for high purposes. It is time for us to speak and work a whole lot harder to this end, so that the winds may blow, the windmills work—and all of us be proud.

# A PROGRAM OF ACTION FOR HIGHER EDUCATION

## David D. Henry

PRESIDENT, UNIVERSITY OF ILLINOIS

THE RANGE AND DEPTH OF THE DISCOURSES ON HIGHER EDUCATION AND the Federal Government, at this Annual Meeting of the American Council on Education, make clear that involvement of the Federal Government in higher education has a long history, that Federal action now affects higher education in many ways, from the flow of students to the nature and quantity of research, and that this involvement is so large, so complex, and so intertwined with the welfare of the nation that it will probably increase.[1]

And yet, most representatives of higher education are critical of the present situation, believing that the Federal expenditures on higher education are uneven, that they are inadequate even for their stated purposes and are not designed to help higher education in any fundamental way meet the demands and opportunities which, in the national interest, should be fulfilled.

For my discussion, I shall assume that the case for increased and more orderly Federal involvement has been made, that the unprecedented anticipated enrollments—which must be accommodated if educational opportunity is not to be curtailed—require unprecedented assistance, that the demands for the specialized competence in research, consultation, and leadership must be met to gird the national interest in science, in the professions, and in many other areas of service, and that these goals, which are essentially national, cannot be reached by the institutions of higher education without increased Federal expenditure.

[1] Suggestive of the involvement of the Federal Government in higher education is the fact that no less than 46 agencies of the Executive Branch now administer programs of importance to higher education.

99

I shall also assume that the effort to enlarge and improve the Federal expenditure upon higher education has not succeeded in ways that the leaders and informed observers believe should have occurred. I will discuss the nature of this failure and make some suggestions for action which we may hope will lead to a better record in the future.

## Slow Progress Is Not Enough

As a starting point, let us look at the record of the Eighty-seventh Congress without reference to the partisan discussions of the moment.

Funds for medical research were increased, but the proposal for full reimbursement of institutional costs was not approved; and the carefully drawn and widely endorsed health professions educational assistance bill did not pass. The College Housing Loan Program was extended and fund authorization increased, but the funds for this self-liquidating housing program, important as have been its benefits, will be fully repaid, with interest. Grants for educational television were authorized, but the total amount involved is disappointingly small.[2] Funds for research, including research facilities, were increased, but the matching requirements remain unrealistic and the reimbursement of indirect costs inadequate. Also listed as "failed to pass" were the proposals for loans and grants for construction of academic facilities and important amendments to the National Defense Education Act. A number of other important proposals could be listed to document the point that higher education did not fare well in the Eighty-seventh Congress.

The failure of the Congress to enact a significant portion of the legislation recommended by the American Council on Education is an index to the task in Federal relations today confronting higher education.

In spite of the well-publicized dissent of a number of institutions and individuals, it may be said that the program of the Council, with reference to the specific measures before the Congress, had a larger consensus than ever before. It may be said, too, that the case for higher education measures was presented to the Congress in hearings and in other ways more clearly and comprehensively than ever before. Not only in

---

[2] *Editor's Note:* Congress in the last few days of the Second Session failed to pass the appropriation bill which included funds for this program.

Washington but also in the states, many college and university staffs, trustees, and institutional friends made efforts to interpret and communicate to the members of Congress their concerns about proposals for Federal legislation affecting higher education.

Some progress in gaining a favorable congressional reaction should be noted, even lacking enactment of the recommended program. This is reflected in the votes of one House or the other, in one committee or another, in the commitment of certain leaders in the Congress and in the executive branch. Nonetheless, in terms of the objectives for meaningful new legislation, modest as they were in scope and cost, "failure" is not too stark a word to employ to describe what happened. At least, news commentators have not hesitated to use such terms as "forgotten proposals" and "politically side-tracked measures."

Since the conditions which precipitated the consensus on the need for Federal action have not changed—indeed, we are one year nearer the day of reckoning with the disastrous consequences of present inadequacies—it is timely that we consider the reasons for our failure and define some guidelines for activity in the days ahead.

Several factors in the failure are readily apparent. First, there is lack of wide recognition, on the part of the general public or in Congress, of the enrollment pressures to come. Even though enrollments in colleges and universities have been increasing during the current low level in the graph of college-age population, few states or regions have come to a true popular understanding of what will be required for the student surge in 1965–1970. The statistics remain an abstraction.

Second, there are those who are skeptical of the social necessity to educate large numbers and who, therefore, are not concerned that educational opportunity is likely to be proportionately less available in the years ahead than in the past.

A third element is the limited time and opportunity for procuring genuine understanding by the members of Congress of the nature and significance of the proposed higher education bills. The problems of higher education are a small portion of the total with which the Congress must deal, and we have not found the way to have those problems become prominent or understood in the main-line decision-making process.

A fourth explanation is the lack of public understanding of the interrelationships between higher education and science, higher education and economic development, and higher education and national morale, and of how higher education is organized.

The general problem in procuring Federal action is cogently and clearly set forth in the new book by Homer Babbidge and Robert Rosenzweig entitled *The Federal Interest in Higher Education*. In my view, this book is a basic text for all who are interested in a better record in Federal legislation for higher education.

It is a historic fact that in the past every Federal action in support of higher education has arisen from a concern to meet the identifiable needs of the national Government, not the needs of higher education per se. Merely to list the topics of specific Federal legislation related to education in recent years makes the point: medical research, housing, urban renewal, national defense, and contracts abroad.

The Federal interest in the welfare of higher education itself has been of so little influence that one might conclude that the Government is willing to impose upon the non-Federal resources of higher education in order to advance the Federal purpose. In no other way can one interpret the refusal to pay full indirect costs on research, full costs of the ROTC, or the extraordinary costs of handling foreign students who are in this country in large numbers as a result of Federal policy. Other examples could be given, including the contribution of faculty services on innumerable panels and committees.

Babbidge and Rosenzweig state, "What is needed from the Government is a point of view toward higher education that includes an end to the notion that institutions of higher education are self-regulating, self-feeding production machines that can be called on indiscriminately to produce goods and services without damage to the mechanism." [3] Indeed, one can make a case that our first effort toward logical Federal–higher education relationships should be to stop higher education aid to the Federal Government!

The incoherent nature of present Federal relations with higher education is a subject in and of itself. Reference to the point is relevant here only to suggest that it is time for the representatives of higher education to recognize clearly the methods of the legislative process and the nature of the historic Federal interest in higher education and mark clearly the steps to be taken in the years ahead.

[3] Babbidge and Rosenzweig, *The Federal Interest in Higher Education* (New York: McGraw-Hill Book Company, 1962), p. 191.

References are frequently made to the fact that the Federal Government is now involved in higher education in the expenditure of several billions of dollars. It is also pointed out that 80 percent of the institutions of higher education in the United States now receive Federal funds, that 20 percent of the total expenditure by higher education comes from the Federal Government [4] and that more than 70 percent of all research conducted by universities is federally financed.[5]

These figures do not mean what they seem to say, however, for twenty institutions in 1959–60 received 79 percent of the total Federal expenditure on higher education and 66 institutions received 92 percent.[6] Thus, in following a policy of not giving support generally to higher education, but for specific purposes instead, great unevenness has developed; indeed, the financial burden of institutions has often been increased by the Federal tasks. The limited and lopsided nature of Federal assistance is further seen in the fact that a great portion of the money spent goes for individuals, not for institutions, and is for highly specialized activities.

The problem of general assistance to higher education has not been confronted in any serious way by the Congress or by the executive departments. Presidents have made speeches on the general importance of higher education, but the administrative practices of their departments and the thrust of their own legislative recommendations have not reflected this approach or concern. Even the facilities bill now before the Congress, on which there is high agreement among all the segments of higher education, envisions an expenditure in grants and loans for facilities of but $300 million a year—when the minimum needed from the Federal Government annually for a period of five years on a one (Federal) to two (local) matching basis, would be at least $750 million.[7] Nor is there a realistic appraisal of where or how the matching requirements are to be met.

[4] Nathan M. Pusey, *Harvard and the Federal Government: A Report to the Faculties and Governing Boards of Harvard University, September 1961* (Cambridge: The University), pp. 1–4.

[5] Homer Babbidge, quoted, *Report,* Occidental College American Assembly, December 1961, p. 8.

[6] Pusey, *op. cit.,* p. 3.

[7] The $750 million figure is computed on a needed total annual expenditure of $2.1 billion—an amount toward the bottom of the range defined by E. V. Hollis, for the decade 1960–70, which begins at an "austerity" level of $16 billion and rises to an "amply justified" $33 billion. (*Higher Education,* XVI [January 1960], 3.)

At the rate of present planning, the closing college door will be shut before Federal assistance in adequate amounts produces the facilities required. It takes three years to plan and build a major structure. Three years from now, in 1965, in most states the curve of college-age population goes sharply upward.

More equitable reimbursement for research overhead, liberalized interest requirements on loans, provision of institutional grants to accompany individual scholarships and grants, loans and matching funds for construction, increased special projects, such as medical research, are all important in their way, but they evade the central issue of adequate support for higher education. They are sporadic, piecemeal, uneven, insufficient.

Alice Rivlin's cogent analysis, *The Role of the Federal Government in Financing Higher Education,* states that Federal policy, or lack of it, is changing, that support of higher education, as such, "is beginning to be recognized as an appropriate federal activity," instead of "a by-product of some other well-established federal concern . . ." [8] But the interval between such a beginning and a firm and adequate policy will be longer than the time available for solutions to the financial problems of the 1960's unless higher education itself is more active than it has been. Miss Rivlin also makes the interesting point that since the Federal Government probably is going to have to relieve the states of some of their growing fiscal burdens in the next ten years, higher education is an appropriate place to give such relief. "This is because of the relation between education and national security," says Miss Rivlin, "because of the interstate mobility of college students and graduates, and because of the national interest in reducing the disparity in opportunities for young people from different parts of the country." [9]

As long as the argument for Federal investment in higher education must follow the historic indirect approach, these points certainly should be considered. Even so, we cannot assume that the Federal interest will naturally evolve in adequate legislative measures without vigorous activity by organized higher education.

My theses, then, are two: first, higher education must increase the effectiveness of its liaison with the Federal Government; and, second,

---

[8] Rivlin, *The Role of the Federal Government in Financing Higher Education* (Washington: Brookings Institution, 1961), p. 118.

[9] *Ibid.,* pp. 154–55.

legislative proposals must be interpreted across the land as well as in Washington.

## The Necessity for Informed Support

Basic to effective legislative action in Washington is greater understanding by the American people of the issues involved and a popular concern for the need for legislation. If the need is properly defined and interpreted, I believe that the American people will respond favorably because, in a sense, we are not talking about the needs of higher education or of institutions; we are talking about the needs of the nation in economic strength, in national defense, in foreign policy, and what higher education can do to fulfill those needs.

In these days of complex national and international life, Congress at times necessarily acts in areas where there is little public understanding of the ultimate significance of the action. Higher education does not fall within this category. Our institutions are local in their history and in their relationships with people. They are a part of the everyday concerns of millions of people. The cumulative significance of higher education to the nation, not now visible to many, will not lead to Government action without popular understanding and encouragement.

We cannot assume that turning to higher education is an inevitable alternative for the Government. However unwise, other courses might be pursued. In research, for example, Government action can establish independent research institutes. Training programs for specialized personnel, even where essentially academic, can be undertaken by Government agencies, as has already been done in the Air Force, in the Army Judge Advocate General's School, and as has been threatened in a number of other areas. Higher education will be increasingly used in the service of the nation only if its program is clearly presented to the American people and to the Government as the most appropriate, the most productive, and the soundest way to fulfill the objectives before the Congress.

I bring full support to Logan Wilson's statement "that Representatives and Senators have said repeatedly that what they most need is what they seldom get—expressions of interest, concern, and judgment from educators known to them in their own districts and states. No matter what steps may be taken to strengthen the Council and other national organizations, no really effective representation for higher education can be achieved in Washington without active involvement by the individual colleges and universities. Thus our task is joint and inseparable." [10]

There are some two thousand higher institutions in the country. Their leadership directly involves faculties and staff, students, parents, alumni, boards of control, and broader constituencies. As a first step in public interpretation of the welfare of higher education, whatever broad consensus is defined can and should be taken directly to this audience of millions. I am not suggesting that our institutional relations be organized as a lobbying effort. I am suggesting, however, that facts, issues, and problems in the area of Federal relations should be clearly understood by our constituencies and discussed by them, so that an informed public opinion will determine what happens, not political laissez faire. The present misrepresentations and misunderstandings must be cleared away.

In the abstract, there is a popular faith in higher education, a feeling for the importance of research and intellectual advancement, an admiration for things cultural and aesthetic, and an almost passionate advocacy of the right of youth to have an opportunity for an education commensurate with talent. We also know that there is some popular sensitivity to the relationship between economic advancement and the education of people, between national defense and trained brain power, between civic health and the preparation of leaders for public service. There is a wide gap, however, between creed and practice, between faith and fulfillment, between appreciation and appropriate action. Collectively, we in higher education have a duty to help bridge that gap.

As a start in clarifying the issues, we should stop referring to "Federal aid" to higher education. From the comments of some opponents to Federal action, one would infer that the Congress is eagerly awaiting an opportunity to appropriate large sums for higher education and through them to take over the direct control of institutions. Anyone who has dealt with this subject in Washington knows how naïve and unrealistic is such a position. Yet "Federal aid to higher education," with vague and sinister implications about Federal control, gets

[10] Logan Wilson, "The Changing Relations of Higher Education and the Federal Government," speech presented at the Annual Conference on Higher Education in Michigan, November 14–15, 1961, University of Michigan, Ann Arbor, 1961, p. 14.

debated while the real issues are overlooked. Debating Federal aid is dealing with a straw man, an irrelevant oversimplification. Instead, we should be asking the American people, "Do you want teachers in your classrooms, doctors at your bedside, lawyers in your courts, scientists in your research laboratories? Are you in favor of having the Federal Government help in the war on cancer and in the evolution of new ideas in the exploration of space? Are you willing to ask the Federal Government to help assure that there will be room for your son or daughter or your grandson or granddaughter on some college campus? Is 'educational security' as important to you as 'social security'?"

These are the terms people must consider. They know that local taxation in most states is near a ceiling, and they know that even in prosperous states the task of finding additional revenues at a time when the Federal Government is talking about tax cuts presents great difficulties to local action. They know that although voluntary giving is at an all-time high and growth is anticipated, philanthropy cannot carry the main load. The public should have the opportunity to react to the relatively modest proposals which have been made for further Federal expenditure, in the relationship of the measures to their personal interests and values and to those of the nation.

There are those who would advocate a broader view in proposing Federal assistance for higher education and would undertake to secure legislation for aid directly to higher education per se, on a plan comparable to the per-student allocation in Canada or to the operation of the University Grants Commission in Great Britain. They would argue from the premise that higher education has a major place in the total economy and national well-being and would seek to have Federal support appropriated directly, without identification of special patterns of Federal concern. They would insist that the present educational practices of the Federal Government "are the product of changing circumstances knitted to old habits of mind and action," [11] and they would seek Federal assistance on the basis of the Government's general obligation for the public welfare. Alice Rivlin classifies the general arguments for such unrestricted subsidy under three categories which might loosely be called social justice, economic growth, and national interest.

[11] Babbidge and Rosenzweig, *op. cit.*, p. 131.

These broad concepts get lip service everywhere. They are the material of speeches by Presidents of the United States, congressional leaders, and civic leaders everywhere. The realities of precedent and political activity, however, undermine the rhetoric. The day may come, indeed, when there will be a Federal policy of assistance for higher education in broad and general terms. In my view, that day is a generation away, and hope for relief in the 1960's must come from specific measures related to the historic pattern of action on Federal concerns.

Meanwhile, as we are forced to follow old paths, we must get the public and the representatives in Congress to understand that aid to individuals is not aid to higher education, whether by scholarships or fellowships or GI benefits or student loan funds; that payments for research are not support of the institution's obligations unless the full costs are paid; and that aid for higher education service to small business, to agriculture, for Government training, for example, while enhancing the usefulness of the institutions, is in no sense aid to higher education in its basic operations.

Further, I believe that a greater effort must be made to isolate the higher education proposals from the controversy surrounding such issues as general aid for elementary-secondary schools, relations of church and state, the Federal responsibility for racial integration, and Federal control of education.

An inadequate Federal Government approach to the problems with which we are here dealing will persist until there is a clear recognition of the national needs and wide support for the proposals offered to help meet them. Time and again, the Federal Government has appropriated funds, whether through public or private agencies, when the national welfare has been involved and a satisfactory formula has been found. In the long history of Federal grants, precedents are ample for support to institutions of higher learning, whether public or private, when they are operating in the national interest. Federal subsidies for agriculture, for transportation, for hospitals, for highways, clearly document the case. History and precedent encourage us in the tasks of public interpretation which confront us.

Time for action is running out, however, and there is the risk that at the peak of the coming enrollment pressure or at the moment of another sputnik, unplanned emergency action may be taken—in a climate of bitterness and recrimination and with the waste of energy and resources usually associated with "crash" programs.

Let us hope that we can avoid such an alternative.

## The Steps Ahead

An essential step in a program for effective action is to enlarge consensus on legislative proposals within higher education and to persuade the dissenters to accept the consensus as far as external action is concerned. It has been no help during the past year to have advocates of legislation which affects a segment or phase of higher education go directly to the Congress with proposals rather than use the educational forums to evolve alignment on a total program. Such activity not only confuses the public and the members of Congress about priorities but also suggests disorganization within the ranks. Moreover, it gives those who are opposed to action an excuse for their opposition.

I firmly believe that the American Council on Education, from its history and present support, has the best opportunity for achieving broad consensus and that the Council machinery should be used to define a legislative program for higher education. To have maximum effectiveness, however, the specialized interests within higher education should keep their debate within the Council and not seek to scuttle Council recommendations or unwittingly take actions which have that effect. Without such professional discipline, a sufficient impact upon the Congress for action cannot be made.

The Council, in turn, must be sensitive to the responsibilities and missions of the organizational members. To receive cooperation from them, the Council staff and leadership must be concerned with their points of view and with helping them in their work. At the point of final decision on program, however, the Council must take responsibility and organize for action in public interpretation.

Again, to quote Babbidge and Rosenzweig, "At some point along the road to maturity and effectiveness, organizations learn the difference between consensus and unanimity, between respect for minority views and immobilization by a minority." [12]

Fred Hechinger points out that "Congress will not listen to occasional academic voices, no matter how distinguished. . . . It was only on the

[12] *Ibid.*, pp. 110–11.

occasions when, out of the chorus of separate voices, a new policy is to be shaped into a harmonious expression of national interest, that the pluralistic desires must be unified, at least to the extent of providing a workable majority." [13]

Apart from the importance of having an influential voice for higher education in major legislative programs, there is the problem of giving technical assistance in legislative matters. Advice to Congress and the executive departments comes from various universities and university people, and the advice is often conflicting, leaving a vacuum of understanding. Such a situation permits strong minorities or individuals to have undue influence. Even uninformed or partially informed people become influential authorities in such situations.

It is also necessary to build more effective liaison and channels of consultation with representatives of other segments of organized education. A very disconcerting episode in the 1962 legislative effort was the formal expression of opposition by six education groups to the legislation proposed by the American Council on Education and its constituent members. That groups representing other educational legislative interests before the Congress, mainly elementary and secondary education, should take concerted action to oppose the main feature of the higher education proposals, namely, aid for the construction of facilities at all colleges, was not a happy circumstance. The spokesmen for these groups undoubtedly feared that a precedent affecting their own proposals would be created by the adoption of the Council-endorsed legislation, but a careful examination of the premises for difference between higher education and elementary-secondary education, as expressed by Government legal authorities and as described by the administration, should at least have been sufficiently reassuring to preclude an action which could do nothing but contribute to legislative inaction.

Unanimity on legislative matters between higher education and elementary-secondary education is probably not to be achieved, but it is not too much to expect sympathetic consultation and communication and the opportunity for exchange of opinion before hurtful public protests are made. It is to be regretted, furthermore, that the public protest by the six education groups referred to was not broadly challenged

[13] Fred Hechinger, "Everybody Says He's for Education, but—," *New York Times Magazine*, July 22, 1962, p. 5.

by spokesmen for higher education, either as to the impropriety of speaking without consultation with those directly affected or as to the substantive assertions made.

The conflict arising from opposition of organized groups in education, outside of higher education, to the proposals for action for colleges and universities must be resolved. If agreement cannot be achieved by discussion, then the public must have direct explanation from higher education that the issues in so-called Federal aid to the public schools and Federal expenditures through higher education have different premises, different historic precedents, and that different purposes and different methods are involved. Those who would put these two programs in one package have not given the total question the thorough attention it must have. This differentiation is not merely a matter of strategy. There are fundamental differences in the two programs, and higher education should make them clear.

Every informed observer on the Washington scene concerned with strengthening education emphasizes that the voice of higher education must be clearer and louder, that there must be a synthesis of viewpoint on proposed legislation, one which all—the Federal departments, the Congress, and higher education—will utilize. The American Council on Education is the one agency which can so serve. Higher education will do itself a service if it fully recognizes this fact and strengthens the Council for its work. The Council, in turn, must accept the responsibility boldly, imaginatively, and aggressively, and find the resources to enable it to build a more effective program.

The main reason for creating the American Council in 1918 was to make available to the Federal agencies the knowledge and judgment of the leadership of American higher education. Partly because of the lack of resources on the part of the Council, partly because of the tremendous growth in institutional relations with the Federal Government, and partly because many other functions were undertaken by the Council, the original purpose became diffused.

Assuming that the Federal relations will be a primary, if not exclusive, concern of the Council in the days ahead, the Council organization must reassert leadership on this front. It must inform its membership on Federal matters, for the Council cannot lead or coordinate unless there is informed understanding of the issues at the institutional level. It must conduct studies as background for recommendation to the Government. It must advise Federal agencies. It must be a legislative counselor. Regional seminars, special publications, and extended field activity are devices to be more widely employed by the Council as resources become available. Specific activity to clarify and gain broad understanding of the Council program must be planned, and follow-up organized.

In carrying out the action program here suggested, the Council obviously must develop an enlarged, highly competent staff in the field of Federal relations to assist in advising on appropriate legislation, to promote a better institutional understanding of what is going on in Washington, and to work with the executive departments as well as the agencies of Congress. Only in this way can the Council attract various groups working on Federal relations into its orbit and sustain the advantages of coordinated activity for all of higher education. All of this will be done in the spirit of interpretation and of contributing to the public debate on vitally important public questions.

There is homework in this assignment for individual Council members as well. If the Council is to have the intelligent support of its members, and if the legislative program is to be broadly interpreted at the local level, individual institutions will have to improve their internal handling of legislative business. I do not believe that presidents and officers associated with presidents can classify Federal relations as a secondary and delegated concern.

Too often the bulletins from the Council are not high-priority reading on the president's desk. Institutional representatives often react to specific issues without any broad understanding of the subjects with which we are here dealing. Sometimes faculty members represent the institution in legislative matters without the knowledge of the president or governing board. Reference has already been made to specialized groups which have presented isolated points of view to the Congress. I am sure that they did so without any intention to harm the success of the general program. The fact that their presentations were used in some instances to defeat Council proposals or modify them in serious ways was not anticipated by them. Very often, the action of these representatives was not known to the heads of their institutions.

Diversity in higher education does not justify a comparable diversity in the relationships to the Federal Government. There are common interests and these common interests must be advanced over the divided ones. Fred R. Cagle, in his study of *Federal Research Projects and the Southern University,* points out that "many faculty members participate in government decisions as members of national advisory committees." Mr. Cagle goes on: "Unfortunately, the university has failed to inculcate in many of these persons an appreciation of the problems of their own institution or of higher education in the United States. These specialists, serving as technical advisors on national committees, may tend to present an extremely narrow view of the university. Although called upon to determine only the technical quality of proposals, such committees are frequently the originators of policies having much influence on the American university." [14]

Lee DuBridge, president of California Institute of Technology, speaks to the same point. "The chief threat of control has come not from the government agencies who administer the funds, but from the panels and advisory committees (composed largely of professors!) who pass upon projects and budgets before they are accepted. Many of these groups have steadfastly opposed proper overhead payments on research contracts, have opposed including allowances for the salaries of professors working on the projects, have opposed block or departmental grants, and have required of the prospective research workers such elaborate and detailed proposals and reports that a type of bureaucratic committee control has grown up which suppresses daring ideas and takes administrative control out of the hands of the universities themselves." [15]

Relatively few college and university leaders are fully aware of the importance of Federal activities to their own institutions, let alone to the structure of higher education in general. Some are totally unaware of such matters. Others, aware of the importance of the issues but not of the significance of their involvement, assume that their interests are adequately represented by a retained Washington agent or, in some vague manner, by the American Council or another national group. Small groups of institutions, parts of institutions, and individuals within institutions have organized themselves into a bewildering con-

[14] Fred R. Cagle, *Federal Research Projects and the Southern University* (Atlanta, Ga.: Southern Regional Education Board, 1962), p. 7.

[15] *Ibid.,* pp. 7–8 (quoted from DuBridge, "Basic Research and the Private University," *Symposium on Basic Research,* American Association for the Advancement of Science, No. 56, 1959, p. 113).

fusion of national organizations with representation in Washington. The results are fragmentation of effort and an uncertain babble of comment that produce lack of confidence, confusion, and some disharmony.

Higher education in America is rightfully proud of its tradition for diversity—diversity in form, purpose, and point of view on nearly all public issues. Debate is vigorous, independent judgments are prized, dissent is respected. To these traits we may attribute much of the vigor of the growth of the acceptance of higher education as a vital part of American life. At the same time we must acknowledge that forward motion in our organizational program has too often been limited by this very diversity and by our habitual expectation that action should be confined to the extent of laissez faire consensus.

Thus, those who speak for higher education have presented divided opinions and positions to Congress, to the Federal executive agencies, and to the home constituencies, and the minimum consensus too often has been the controlling influence in defining a program for joint action. Further, the capacity for leadership and support of a national program of action for higher education has not been fully organized and utilized, either at the local or national level.

Such a condition is not enough for what must now be done. It is time to improve the machinery for decision on higher education issues and work together for the implementation of the judgments made. We cannot expect unanimity or even broad consensus always to be a prerequisite to action. We must count on representative leadership to lead without a referendum on every position to be taken or a poll on every proposal.

At the moment, education in American life is seen in bits and pieces, in segments and fractions. National improvement, cumulatively at the local level as well as in Federal legislation, will come only when the education function and service as a whole come into focus, in a coherent and unified pattern.

The American Council on Education, as the only organization representing all types of institutions of higher education, must take the initiative in awakening a greater awareness of the issues involved. More, it must seek to educate educators to the importance of what is now being done and of what is in prospect and attempt to bring consensus out of the varying expressions of different groups and different positions. It must offer recommendations on Federal policies that will serve the best interests of higher education and represent these policies before the Government. It must do so, furthermore, out of its own responsibility for intelligent and responsible action.

Just as each institution and each constituent member here represented must consider ways and means of identifying its work with the overriding national and international issues of our time, so must the American Council on Education, representing all of us, find new ways to heightened effectiveness in giving a coherent national view of our institutions and their services, in aggressively representing us in the struggle for additional resources and in giving leadership to the mutual strengthening of all for the tasks at hand.

Admittedly, the suggestions for action which I have made deal with the immediate future, the short range. This is not to suggest that higher education, along with others, should not continue to debate national goals and the relationship of higher education to them. Indeed, as has been pointed out, it is because such national goals have not been defined for higher education and accepted that we are faced with the present indecision, inadequacies, and lack of national plan. However, time has run out and we have no choice but to follow the course of expediency and attachment to precedent while a more clear-cut, overall national policy is being evolved.

Planning has been widely accepted as essential for individual institutions, for state and regional programs in higher education. It is also essential for the nation as a whole and for the Federal Government in the area of education relationships.

To the end of evolving broad objectives and procuring agreement upon them, as they apply to the national welfare, it is vital that the long-recommended suggestion of the American Council on Education for the creation of a board of presidential advisers on education receive immediate attention. It is something of an anomaly that a presidential science committee was created before one was created for education, that the posture of the Government hence reflects education as a part of science, rather than science as a part of education, and that this committee has been the chief voice to the Federal Government on the Government's relationships to science education.

Many commissions, task forces, national conferences, and organizations have brought support to the idea of a council of educational advisers to the President in some form. Certainly a maximum national effort for the strengthening of education will not be possible until the American people and their Government have a comprehensive, objective, multidimensional view of their schools, how they are related to the national interest, and what specific means for strengthening them are in order. A board of presidential advisers, unfettered by politics and unencumbered by administrative authority or responsibility, is the simplest and most promising means to that end.

## *Conclusion*

At a time of increasing competition for the tax dollar and the philanthropic gift, and at a time of increasing public concern at the level of public expenditure, citizens everywhere are confronted with the decision of how to pay the educational price for our standard of living and our national security and how and in what way that price is to be paid. It is not enough that people applaud the idea of educational opportunity, educational standards of quality, and intellectual advancement, including research; it is essential that ways and means be found to pay for them, and the Federal Government must assume its share of the responsibility.

The Federal Government must appraise its obligation for higher education, and the American Council on Education has a central place in stimulating such action and in advising as to the most effective response to it.

We must strive for a condition, says John Gardner of the Carnegie Corporation, which would have education as "our national preoccupation, our passion, our obsession." [16] The schools and colleges would then be the heart of a national endeavor, not, as Mr. Gardner says they now often find themselves, "swimming upstream against the interests of a public that thinks everything else more urgent." [17] We are held back not by lack of capacity or power. Our choices, not our means, will be decisive. As a people, we can accomplish what we set out to do.

---

[16] John W. Gardner, "The Servant of All Our Purposes," The Carnegie Corporation of New York *Annual Report* (New York: The Corporation, 1958), p. 15.
[17] *Ibid.*, p. 17.

# SELECTED BIBLIOGRAPHY

## I. GENERAL

AMERICAN ASSEMBLY. *The Federal Government and Higher Education.* Ed. Douglas Knight. Englewood Cliffs, N.J.: Prentice-Hall, Inc., 1960. ix + 205 pp. Cloth, $3.50; paper, $1.95.

Contains background papers prepared for the Seventeenth American Assembly, held at Arden House, May 5–8, as well as the final report adopted by the Assembly. The reports of the several Regional Assemblies, conducted in the aftermath of the National Assembly, also contain valuable insights and summaries of opinion on this subject. Regional Assemblies were conducted under the auspices of Occidental College, Saint Louis University, Tulane University, University of Minnesota, University of New Mexico, and University of Oregon.

AMERICAN COLLEGE PUBLIC RELATIONS ASSOCIATION. *Federal Government Programs for Colleges and Universities: Papers, Remarks and Questions from Conferences of November 20–21 and December 11–12, 1961, of the American College Public Relations Association in Washington, D.C.* Washington: The Association, 1962. xi + 161 pp. $5.00.

Valuable principally for its descriptions of current Federal programs affecting higher education, as presented by administrators of those programs.

AXT, RICHARD G. *The Federal Government and Financing Higher Education.* New York: Columbia University Press, 1952. O.P. xiv + 295 pp.

One of the earliest general explorations of the growing role of the Federal Government, and the problems beginning to emerge therefrom.

BABBIDGE, HOMER D., JR., and ROSENZWEIG, ROBERT M. *The Federal Interest in Higher Education.* New York: McGraw-Hill Book Co., 1962. viii + 214 pp. $5.95.

An extended analytical essay on the political and educational dynamics of the relationship between the Federal Government and higher education. Discusses related issues of public policy and prospects for future developments.

BOWEN, WILLIAM G. *The Federal Government and Princeton University: A Report on the Effects of Princeton's Involvements with the*

*Federal Government on the Operations of the University.* Privately published, Princeton University, January 1962. xiv + 319 pp.

Circulation of this excellent self-study is closely limited. Copies are *not* available from Princeton.

CARNEGIE FOUNDATION FOR THE ADVANCEMENT OF TEACHING. *Federal Programs in Higher Education: Summary of a Discussion by the Trustees of the Carnegie Foundation for the Advancement of Teaching.* Reprinted from the 1956–1957 Annual Report. New York: The Foundation, n.d. 20 pp.

An early but still timely and concise treatment of the general subject.

————. "Higher Education and the Federal Government." MS in preparation.

Report of a survey, directed by Reuben H. Gross, of the Federal Government and higher education, including the impact of Federal programs as revealed in a series of institutional self-studies.

*Harvard and the Federal Government: A Report to the Faculties and Governing Board of Harvard University.* Cambridge, Mass.: Harvard University, 1961. 36 pp.

The first comprehensive self-study by a university of the effects of its involvement with the Federal Government.

ORLANS, HAROLD. *The Effects of Federal Programs on Higher Education: A Report to the U.S. Commissioner of Education.* Draft edition; multilithed. Washington: Brookings Institution, 1962. O.P. xix + 408 pp. Printed edition to be published by Brookings, about October 1962; 300 pp. (est.).

A study of the impact of Federal programs on a selected, representative group of institutions, undertaken for the U.S. Commissioner of Education, under authority of title X of the National Defense Education Act.

RIVLIN, ALICE M. *The Role of the Federal Government in Financing Higher Education.* Washington: Brookings Institution, 1961. xii + 179 pp. Cloth, $3.00; paper, $2.00.

Traces the growing role of Federal funds in financing higher education, and analyzes the past, present, and possible future patterns of such support.

U.S. LIBRARY OF CONGRESS. LEGISLATIVE REFERENCE SERVICE. *The Historic and Current Federal Role in Education: A Report to the*

*Subcommittee on Education of the Committee on Labor and Public Welfare, United States Senate* . . . Printed for the use of the Committee on Labor and Public Welfare. 87th Cong., 1st Sess. Washington: Government Printing Office, 1961. vi + 66 pp. Free upon request to Senate Committee on Labor and Public Welfare.

A background document prepared for the Senate Committee on Labor and Public Welfare on the eve of the hectic 1961 session on educational legislation.

————. [Prepared] by Charles A. Quattlebaum. *Federal Educational Policies, Programs and Proposals: A Survey and Handbook.* Part I: *Background; Issues; Relevant Considerations.* Part II: *Survey of Federal Educational Activities.* Part III: *Analyses and Classification of Programs.* Printed for the use of the Committee on Education and Labor, U.S. House of Representatives. 86th Cong., 2d Sess. Washington: Government Printing Office, 1960. O.P. I: viii + 192. II: xv + 372. III: xvi + 234.

The most extensive catalogue of the historical and current facts of Federal programs in education.

U.S. OFFICE OF EDUCATION. *Federal Funds for Education: Fields, Levels, Recipients, 1959 and 1960.* By Penrose B. Jackson and Dolores A. Steinhilber. OE-10013. Circular No. 679. Washington: Government Printing Office, 1962. ix + 82. $0.60.

Represents a refinement of the earlier biennial Office of Education publication, *Federal Funds for Education.* A comprehensive report of Federal expenditures in educational programs.

————. *A Survey of Federal Programs in Higher Education—Final Report.* By J. Kenneth Little. OE-50034. Bulletin 1963, No. 6. In press. Washington: Government Printing Office, about October 1962. 200 pp. (est.).

The report of a survey undertaken by Dr. Little for the U.S. Office of Education, under authority of title X of the National Defense Education Act.

*A Survey of Federal Programs in Higher Education—Summary* (OE-50033; 56 pp.) was published and widely distributed by the Office of Education in September. This summary contains a brief not only of the survey undertaken by Dr. Little, but also of the Orlans study (see above) and the recommendations formulated by Dr. Little. In general, this summary describes the variety of the federally sponsored programs and the character and relative involvement of the participating institutions of higher education, with the primary purpose of assessing the impact of Federal programs on these institutions.

## II.  SCIENCE AND SPONSORED RESEARCH

AMERICAN COUNCIL ON EDUCATION. *Sponsored Research Policy of Colleges and Universities: A Report of the Committee on Institutional Research Policy.* Washington: The Council, 1954. vii + 93 pp. $1.50.

A report on issues involved in sponsored research designed to guide educational institutions in forming policies which collectively bring about improved relationships with Government agencies, foundations, and industry.

BUSH, VANNEVAR. *Science, The Endless Frontier: A Report to the President on a Program for Postwar Scientific Research.* Washington: National Science Foundation, July 1945; reprinted July 1960 [with an Introduction by Alan T. Waterman]. xxvi + 220 pp. Limited number of copies available free on request.

A document of historical importance which presents an authoritative assessment of science and medicine in World War II, together with a blueprint for their postwar development.

CAGLE, FRED R. *Federal Research Projects and the Southern University.* Atlanta, Ga.: Southern Regional Education Board, 1962. iii + 97 pp.

A study of the influence of Federal research projects on a group of Southern universities with the general objective of providing a perspective on problems created by the availability of Federal funds for project research, the reaction of universities to such problems, and needed policies.

DUPRÉ, J. STEFAN, and LAKOFF, SANFORD A. *Science and the Nation.* Englewood Cliffs, N.J.: Prentice-Hall, Inc., 1962. 181 pp. Cloth, $3.95; paper, $1.95.

Attempts to provide a concise survey of developments related to "the impact of science upon social thought and the role of technology in industrial societies," including the formulation of United States science policy and the political activity of scientists.

DUPREE, A. HUNTER. *Science in the Federal Government: A History of Policies and Activities to 1940.* Cambridge, Mass.: Belknap Press of Harvard University Press, 1957. xii + 460 pp. $7.50.

Traces "the development of the policies and activities of the United States government in science from the establishment of the federal Constitution to the year 1940."

EXECUTIVE OFFICE OF THE PRESIDENT. BUREAU OF THE BUDGET. *Report to the President on Government Contracting for Research and Development.* Prepared by the Bureau of the Budget and Referred to the Committee on Government Operations, United States Senate. Senate Doc. No. 94. 87th Cong., 2d Sess. Washington: Government Printing Office, 1962. xiii + 92 pp. Free on request to Senate Document Room, U.S. Congress, Washington 25, D.C.

A review of the experience of the Government in using contracts with private institutions and enterprises to obtain research and development work needed for public purposes. The "Bell Report."

KIDD, CHARLES V. *American Universities and Federal Research.* Cambridge, Mass.: Belknap Press of Harvard University Press, 1959. xiv + 272 pp. $6.00.

"The central thesis of this book is that large-scale Federal financing of research has set in motion irreversible forces that are affecting the nature of universities, altering their capacity to teach, changing their financial status, modifying the character of parts of the Federal administrative structure, establishing new political relations, and changing the way research itself is organized." Still a landmark study.

MICHIGAN STATE UNIVERSITY. OFFICE OF RESEARCH DEVELOPMENT AND THE GRADUATE SCHOOL. *Sponsored Research: Significance and Basic Characteristics; Policies and Procedures at Michigan State University; Preparation of Proposals and Selected Sources of Support.* East Lansing: The University, 1961. vi + 126 pp.

An "attempt to define the dimensions of the problem of sponsored research as a national phenomenon and as applied to Michigan State University." Includes information on policies and procedures of the university, preparation of proposals, and services developed to assist the faculty on sponsored research problems.

NATIONAL SCIENCE FOUNDATION. *Basic Research: A National Resource.* NSF 57–35. Washington: Government Printing Office, 1957. viii + 64 pp. $0.45.

A report "designed to convey in nontechnical language the meaning of basic research in science and how important it is to the Nation in its concern for its economy, the health of its citizens, and its defense."

———. *Federal Funds for Science X: Fiscal Years 1960, 1961, and 1962.* NSF 61–82. Washington: Government Printing Office, 1962. vii + 145 pp. $0.75.

Presents and analyzes the Federal funds provided for research and development and research and development plant.

————. *Government-University Relationships in Federally Sponsored Scientific Research and Development.* NSF 58–10. Washington: Government Printing Office, 1958. ix + 44 pp. $0.40.

Describes the "evolution of Federal sponsorship of research and development at colleges and universities and indicate[s] the current nature, trends, and magnitude of this financial support."

"'Perspectives on Government and Science," [issue] edited by Norman Wengert, *Annals of the American Academy of Political and Social Science, CCCXXVII,* January 1960. x + 138.

This complete issue of *The Annals* is devoted to Government and science. Articles are grouped under three major classifications: "Needs, Problems, Opportunities," "Administration of Government Science," and "Government Science and the Universities."

PRESIDENT'S SCIENTIFIC RESEARCH BOARD. *Report of the President's Scientific Research Board: Science and Public Policy.* Washington: Government Printing Office, 1947. 5 vols. O.P.

The Steelman Report. A broad evaluation of the nation's scientific activities, including organization, manpower, resources, and medical research.

PRICE, DON K. *Government and Science: Their Dynamic Relation in American Democracy.* New York: New York University Press, 1954. viii + 203 pp. $3.75.

The significant effect of scientists on the nature of the American governmental system. Originally presented as a series of lectures at New York University.

*Scientific Progress, the Universities, and the Federal Government: Statement by the President's Science Advisory Committee.* Washington: Government Printing Office, 1960. v + 33 pp. $0.15.

The widely noted "Seaborg Report." Its focus is on problems associated with "the advancement of science by basic research, and the making of scientists by graduate education."

*Strengthening American Science: A Report of the President's Science Advisory Committee.* [With] a Statement by the President. Washington: Government Printing Office, 1958. iii + 36 pp. $0.20.

A policy statement on ways the Federal Government could best help strengthen American science and technology as essential resources for national security and welfare. Includes recommendation to establish a Federal Council for Science and Technology.

WOLFLE, DAEL. *Science and Public Policy.* Lincoln: University of Nebraska Press, 1959. vi + 81 pp. $1.50.

A series of lectures by the executive officer of the American Association for the Advancement of Science, presented at the University of Nebraska. Chap. 2, "Science in the Federal Government," is a concise introduction to the subject. Also includes: "Science and Public Policy" and "Education in a World of Science."

## III. COMMISSION REPORTS

ALLEN, HOLLIS P. *The Federal Government and Education.* New York: McGraw-Hill Book Co., 1950. O.P. xvii + 333 pp.

"The original and complete study of education for the Hoover Commission Task Force on Public Welfare."

COMMISSION ON INTERGOVERNMENTAL RELATIONS. *A Report to the President for Transmittal to the Government.* Washington: Government Printing Office, 1955. O.P. xi + 311 pp. $1.25.

The summary report of the Commission. Published separately are reports of the Commission's several study committees. Of special interest are the Study Committee Reports on *Federal Responsibility in the Field of Education* (Washington: Government Printing Office, 1955; $0.50) and *Federal Aid to Agriculture* (Washington: Government Printing Office, 1955; $0.20).

PRESIDENT'S COMMISSION ON HIGHER EDUCATION. *Higher Education for American Democracy.* Washington: Government Printing Office, 1947. 6 vols. O.P. New York: Harper & Bros., 1947. O.P.

Report of President Truman's Commission, headed by George F. Zook. Vol. 3, chap. 4, and Vol. 5, chap. 4, especially, deal with the Federal Government's involvement in higher education.

PRESIDENT'S COMMITTEE ON EDUCATION BEYOND THE HIGH SCHOOL. *Second Report to the President.* Washington: Government Printing Office, 1957. xiii + 108 pp. $0.55.

The final report of the Josephs Committee, appointed by President Eisenhower. Its concluding chapter deals specifically with the role of the Federal Government in postsecondary education. A summary of the report was issued at the same time; xiii + 26 pp.

## IV.  SPECIFIC PROGRAMS

### A.  Land-Grant Institutions

EDDY, EDWARD D., JR. *Colleges for Our Land and Time: The Land-Grant Idea in American Education.* New York: Harper & Bros., 1957. xiv + 328 pp. $4.50.

ROSS, EARLE D. *Democracy's Colleges: The Land-Grant Movement in the Formative Stage.* Ames: Iowa State University Press, 1942. O.P.

U.S. OFFICE OF EDUCATION. *Land-Grant Colleges and Universities, 1862–1962.* By Henry S. Brunner. OE-50030. Bulletin 1962, No. 13. Washington: Government Printing Office, 1962. viii + 78 pp. $0.35.

Contains the basic Federal laws and rulings of the land-grant system, a chronology of institutions, and bibliography.

### B.  Agriculture

BLISS, R. B. (compiler and ed.). *The Spirit and Philosophy of Extension Work.* Washington: Graduate School, U.S. Department of Agriculture, and Epsilon Sigma Phi [national honorary extension fraternity]. O.P. x + 393 pp.

TRUE, ALFRED CHARLES. *A History of Agricultural Education in the U.S.* U.S. Department of Agriculture Misc. Pub. No. 36, 1928. O.P.

———. *A History of Agricultural Experimentation and Research in the U.S.* U.S. Department of Agriculture Misc. Pub. No. 251, 1937. O.P.

———. *A History of Agricultural Extension Work in the U.S.* U.S. Department of Agriculture Misc. Pub. No. 15, 1928. O.P.

U.S. DEPARTMENT OF AGRICULTURE. COOPERATIVE STATE EXPERIMENT STATION SERVICE. *A History of Research Policy and Procedure.* By H. C. Knoblauch, E. M. Law, and W. P. Meyer. U.S. Department of Agriculture Misc. Pub. No. 904. Washington: Government Printing Office, May 1962. vi + 262 pp. $1.50.

## C. Medical Education and Research

COMMITTEE OF MEDICAL CONSULTANTS ON MEDICAL RESEARCH. *Federal Support of Medical Research.* Washington: Government Printing Office, 1960. xxix + 133 pp. $0.75.

A report prepared for the Senate Committee on Appropriations, dealing principally with the scope of activities and needs of the National Institutes of Health.

KREISBERG, LOUIS, and ROSENBERG, LARRY. *The Impact of Federal Grants on Medical Education: An Essay and an Annotated Bibliography.* Mimeographed. New York: National Opinion Research Center, 1959(?). O.P.

U.S. DEPARTMENT OF HEALTH, EDUCATION, AND WELFARE. *The Advancement of Medical Research and Education through the Department of Health, Education, and Welfare: Final Report of the Secretary's Consultants on Medical Research and Education.* Washington: Government Printing Office, 1958. 82 pp. $0.60.

The Bayne-Jones report on current and recommended programs of the Department of Health, Education, and Welfare in the area of medical education and research.

## D. ROTC

LYONS, GENE M., and MASLAND, JOHN W. *Education and Military Leadership: A Study of the ROTC.* Princeton, N.J.: Princeton University Press, 1959. xvii + 283 pp. $5.00.

MASLAND, JOHN W., and RADWAY, LAURENCE I. *Soldiers and Scholars: Military Education and National Policy.* Princeton, N.J.: Princeton University Press, 1957. 530 pp. $7.50.

## E. International Programs

FORD FOUNDATION. COMMITTEE ON THE UNIVERSITY AND WORLD AFFAIRS. *The University and World Affairs.* New York: The Foundation, 1960. vi + 84 pp. Free.

U.S. HOUSE OF REPRESENTATIVES. COMMITTEE ON GOVERNMENT OPERATIONS. *Government Programs in International Education (A Survey and Handbook). Forty-second Report by the Committee on Government Operations.* [Principal author, Charles A. Quattlebaum.] 85th Cong., 2d Sess., House Report No. 2712. Washington: Government Printing Office, 1959. O.P. x + 251 pp.

## V.    RELATED ISSUES OF PUBLIC POLICY

NATIONAL CATHOLIC WELFARE CONFERENCE. LEGAL DEPARTMENT. *The Constitutionality of the Inclusion of Church-Related Schools in Federal Aid to Education.* A reprint from *Georgetown Law Journal,* L (Winter 1961), 399–455. Available from National Catholic Welfare Conference, 1312 Massachusetts Ave., N.W., Washington 5, D.C.

U.S. COMMISSION ON CIVIL RIGHTS. *Equal Protection of the Laws in Public Higher Education, 1960.* Washington: Government Printing Office, 1961. xv + 355 pp. $1.00.

An extensive review of Federal programs and their administration in the light of racial policies of public institutions of higher education.

U.S. SENATE. *Constitutionality of Federal Aid to Education in Its Various Aspects.* 87th Cong., 1st Sess., Senate Document No. 29. May 1, 1961. Washington: Government Printing Office, 1961. O.P. vi + 72 pp.

A summary of legal views, centering largely on the church-state issue. It includes the memorandum on constitutionality of aid to church-related institutions prepared by General Counsel of the Department of Health, Education, and Welfare.

# AMERICAN COUNCIL ON EDUCATION

The American Council on Education is a *council* of educational organizations and institutions, founded in 1918. Its purpose is to advance education and educational methods through comprehensive voluntary and cooperative action on the part of American higher educational associations, organizations, and institutions.

## EXECUTIVE OFFICERS

LOGAN WILSON, President

ALLAN M. CARTTER, Vice-President; Director, Commission on Plans and Objectives

LAWRENCE E. DENNIS, Director, Commission on Academic Affairs

CHARLES G. DOBBINS, Assistant to the President; Director, Commission on Federal Relations

RICHARD A. HUMPHREY, Director, Commission on International Education

FRED S. VORSANGER, Treasurer and Business Manager

CHARLES H. WATTS, Director, Commission on Administrative Affairs

## ADMINISTRATIVE STAFF

C. H. WALTER HOWE, Staff Associate

HELEN C. HURLEY, Librarian

EARL W. LINDVEIT, Staff Associate

WILLIAM A. MILLER, JR., Staff Associate

OLIVE MILLS, Production Editor

ROBERT QUICK, Director of Publications

ELEANOR QUILL, Secretary to the President

HARRISON SASSCER, Staff Associate

DOROTHY R. SMITH, Staff Assistant

## PROJECT DIRECTORS

FREDERICK R. MANGOLD, Leaders and Specialists

JOSEPH M. TROXELL, Inter-American Schools Service

CORNELIUS P. TURNER, Accreditation of Service Experiences

ELMER D. WEST, Statistical Information and Research